Move 37

The Life of Demis Hassabis

Paul D Johnson

Copyright © 2026 by Paul D. Johnson

All rights reserved.

No portion of this book may be reproduced in any form without written permission from the publisher or author, except as permitted by U.S. copyright law.

This manuscript was generated with the assistance of artificial intelligence. See "A Note on How This Book Was Written" for details.

Cover photograph by Christopher Michel, licensed under CC BY-SA 4.0. Source: Wikimedia Commons.

Contents

For everyone who ever played Theme Park and wondered what happened to the kid who made it.

"If you're building a mind more powerful than any human mind, what happens when you succeed?"

Chapter One

The Resignation

*C*_ _ _ _ *hildhood, Chess, and the Epiphany in Liechtenstein*

The boy was eleven years old, and he had been playing chess for ten hours.

It was an international tournament near Liechtenstein, in a huge hall filled with hundreds of players from across Europe. His opponent was the Danish champion, a grown man in his thirties or forties. The boy had a king and a queen. The Dane had a king, a rook, a bishop, and a knight. On paper, the Dane held the advantage, but in practice, the position should have been a draw. For four hours, the man had been probing and manoeuvring, trying to find a crack. The other games had ended long ago. The hall had emptied around them. Still, they played.

Finally, the Dane found what he was looking for. He set a trap, boxing the boy's king into a corner where checkmate appeared inevitable. There was one way out. All the boy had to do was sacrifice his queen—give it away for nothing—and the result would be stalemate. A draw. The correct outcome. But the boy was eleven, and exhausted. He had been sitting in a chair for the better part of a day. His mind, which had been running at full capacity for longer than most adults would tolerate, was no longer working the way it needed to. He did not see the sacrifice. Staring at his trapped king, he assumed the position was lost. He resigned.

The Dane stood up. His friends were gathered around him, and he laughed. Then he looked down at the board and asked the boy why he had given up. It was a draw. With a casual flourish, the man demonstrated the move the boy had missed. The sacrifice of the queen. The stalemate. The draw that had been sitting there all along, waiting to be found.

The injustice of the moment stayed with the boy. The man had tried a cheap trick on a child, and it had worked. Twelve hours of grinding effort had produced nothing. But what stayed with him even longer was the thought that came next, as he walked back through the hall and past the other players, past all those brilliant minds bent over boards, past all that ferocious intelligence deployed in the service of a game.

"Are we wasting our minds?" he asked himself. He looked at the players around him, all of them formidably smart, and thought: what if all that brainpower were put to use on something more urgent? What if, instead of spending their lives finding the perfect move, they were trying to cure cancer or solve some disease?

He was eleven years old. He would later call it an epiphany. It would change the direction of his life and, in time, change the direction of science.

• • •

Demis Hassabis was born on July 27, 1976, in London. His father, Costas, was a Greek Cypriot. His mother, Angela, was a Chinese Singaporean. Both were teachers. They lived in North London, in Finchley, and they raised their three children in a household that Hassabis would later describe, when pressed for a single word, as bohemian.

Costas had been a singer-songwriter in his youth and had moved through a variety of creative jobs. For a time, the family ran a toy shop. They were not wealthy or academic. They followed their interests wherever those interests led, and they gave their children the same permission. You did not have to be constricted by convention. You could explore your own path deeply, and that was not merely acceptable but the right way to live.

The household produced three unusual children. His sister became a pianist and composer. His brother became a professional poker player. Hassabis went in an entirely different direction, toward mathematics and science and computers, and he was never quite sure where the impulse came from. His parents were self-described technophobes. Neither of his siblings shared his scientific bent. Something in his wiring was simply different.

But the toy shop left a mark. The family would bring home the board games that couldn't be sold because they had pieces missing. Boxes without all their components. Games without rules. Demis would take them, invent replacement rules from scratch, and then play the results with his younger brother and sister, who served, unknowingly, as his first game testers. He would watch what worked and what didn't, refine the designs, and try again. It was, he later realised, his first education in game design. It was also, though he could not have known it at the time, his first lesson in the thing he would spend his life pursuing: the design of systems that learn through experience.

• • •

He discovered chess at the age of four. His father was playing a game against an uncle, and the boy watched. Within two weeks, he was beating adults.

By five, he was competing nationally. At six, he won the London under-eights championship. By nine, he was captaining the England under-eleven team. At thirteen, he reached master standard, with an Elo rating of 2,300. By the time he was twelve, he was the second-highest-rated chess player in the world for his age.

His father had pulled him out of school for stretches so he could focus on tournaments. The family travelled across Europe. Looking back, Hassabis could barely remember doing any schoolwork from that period. It was all chess. The rest of life existed in the background, a blur of hotel rooms and tournament halls and the particular silence that descends on a room full of people thinking as hard as they can.

He attended Queen Elizabeth's School in Barnet, a selective state school in North London, from 1988 to 1990. There followed a period of homeschooling—his parents were bohemian, unconventional, and saw no reason to be constricted by the usual path. He then moved to Christ's College in Finchley, where he sat his A-level exams—the rigorous subject-specific examinations that determine university entry in England—two years early, at sixteen: double maths, physics, and chemistry. He was offered a place at Queens' College, Cambridge, to study computer science but was told he was too young to take it up immediately. He would have to wait a year. In the meantime, he would need something to do.

But first there was the matter of chess. The tournament near Liechtenstein happened when he was eleven. The resignation, the Dane's laugh, the empty hall. After that, something shifted. He kept playing. He captained the Cambridge varsity chess team for three years running, winning a half blue—a university sporting honour, one step below the full blue awarded for the most competitive sports. He would go on to compete in all manner of mental contests, winning the Pentamind championship at the Mind Sports Olympiad a record five times between 1998 and 2003. He won a Diplomacy world team championship. He cashed in the World Series of Poker six times. The competitive drive never left him. But after Liechtenstein, he knew that chess alone would not be enough. The brilliant minds in that hall deserved a better problem.

• • •

The first computer arrived when he was eight. It was a ZX Spectrum 48K, the cheap black slab of plastic with rubber keys that introduced a generation of British children to programming. Hassabis bought it with two hundred pounds he had won at a chess tournament.

He taught himself to code from books. He and his father would visit Foyles, the legendary bookshop on Charing Cross Road, and sit in the computing section for hours. One book in particular changed things. It was called The Chess Computer Handbook, by David Levy, and it explained in full detail how chess programs were made—the search trees, the evaluation functions, the technique called alpha-beta pruning that allowed a machine to discard bad moves without examining them. For a boy who had spent his life playing chess against human opponents, the book was a revelation. It showed him that the game he knew intuitively could be translated into algorithms. It was a bridge between two worlds he loved: the world of the board and the world of the machine.

He later recalled those early computing years with an almost spiritual reverence: the computer was, to him, a device that could extend the reach of a human mind, a machine that kept working even after you went to sleep, a tool that felt magical in its capacity to amplify thought.

The physicist Richard Feynman had said that what he could not build, he could not understand. Hassabis discovered the same principle from the opposite direction. By building things on the computer—first simple programs, then games, then crude simulations—he began to understand how systems worked. And the computer had a property that thrilled him in a way that chess never quite could. You could set it running on a problem. You could walk away, go to bed. In the morning the answer would be waiting. For a boy who was already thinking about intelligence itself, this was intoxicating. It was as if the machine could think on your behalf.

The Spectrum gave way to a Commodore Amiga, a more powerful machine, and the hobby deepened. Hassabis and a couple of school friends formed what amounted to a hacking club. They would compete with each other writing assembly code, making visual demos, building small games. All his spare time went into programming. The world of computers felt, he later said, like a secret. A hidden world that almost nobody else knew existed.

On the Amiga, he wrote his first artificial intelligence program. It played the board game Reversi—a simpler game than chess, but complex enough to be interesting. He used all the principles he had learned from Levy's book: alpha-beta search, position evaluation, the systematic pruning of bad moves. A boy of eleven or twelve, sitting in his bedroom in Finchley, writing software that could play a strategy game against a human opponent. Not because anyone had assigned it. Not for school. Because it was the most interesting thing he could think of doing. The thread that would run through his entire life—games as the labouratory for intelligence, computers as the tool for building it—was already visible.

. . .

The other formative experience arrived through a screen. He was a teenager when he first saw Ridley Scott's Blade Runner, the 1982 science fiction film in which artificial beings are indistinguishable from humans. The film ends with a dying replicant delivering a monologue about the experiences he has accumulated, memories that will vanish when he dies.

Hassabis was transfixed. He would later say that Blade Runner brought artificial intelligence to life for him in a way nothing else had. The film did not merely present AI as a technical concept. It presented it as a question about the nature of the mind, about what makes a memory, about what it means to be conscious. These were the questions that already fascinated him, and the film showed him they were not just scientific puzzles but the deepest questions a person could ask. He chose a piece of the Vangelis soundtrack from Blade Runner as one of his most treasured records, saying he could think about its themes for a lifetime.

It is worth pausing here, because the teenager who watched Blade Runner was not an ordinary filmgoer encountering science fiction for the first time. He was a chess master who had already written an AI program. He had already experienced the revelation in Liechtenstein. He had already intuited, however vaguely, that intelligence itself was the real problem worth solving. The film did not plant the idea. It gave the idea its emotional shape. It showed him that the work he was being drawn toward touched something more than mathematics. It touched the question of what it means to be alive.

. . .

He was sixteen when Cambridge told him to wait a year. Most teenagers in his position might have travelled. Hassabis did something more characteristic. He entered a national competition in Amiga Power magazine, in which the grand prize was a job at Bullfrog Productions, a celebrated game studio in Guildford run by the legendary designer Peter Molyneux. Hassabis had been obsessed with one of Bullfrog's games, a simulation called Populous, since he was twelve. He entered the competition and came second. But second was close enough. He rang Molyneux's office and asked if he could come for work experience. Molyneux agreed.

The day after his final exam, he took the train to Guildford.

What happened there would make him famous in the gaming world before he was old enough to vote. But that is a story for the next chapter.

For now, the important thing is the decision that preceded everything else. Sometime around his eleventh birthday, in the aftermath of the tournament near Liechtenstein, Demis Hassabis told his parents he did not intend to become a professional chess player. They were stunned. He was the second-highest-rated player in the world for his age. Everyone around him assumed that chess was his destiny. His whole life, so far as he could remember it, had been chess.

He walked away from it anyway. The reason, he said, was simple: "It didn't feel productive enough somehow."

It was a remarkable thing for a child to conclude, and a more remarkable thing for a child to act on. Most prodigies are consumed by the discipline that made them prodigies. They follow the path of least resistance, which is also the path of greatest applause. Hassabis did the opposite. He examined the thing he was best at in the world—the thing that earned him recognition and trophies and an identity—and decided it was not enough. The minds in that hall deserved a harder problem.

He would spend the next three decades searching for one. He would design games and build simulated worlds. He would study the human brain and map the neural machinery of memory and imagination. He would start a company devoted to a five-word mission statement and sell it to the most powerful technology company on earth. He would teach a machine to play the most complex board game in history and then, when that was done, turn the same technology loose on a fifty-year-old mystery about the building blocks of life. He would win a Nobel Prize.

And through all of it, the question that had formed in the mind of an exhausted eleven-year-old in a town hall near Liechtenstein would remain the animating question of his career: What if all that intelligence could be used for something that actually mattered? What if intelligence itself could be understood, replicated, and deployed as a tool?

He had a phrase for what he was looking for. He called it a meta-solution—a solution to the problem of solving problems. Intelligence as the master key. The thing that unlocks everything else.

He was going to try to build it.

Chapter Two

Theme Park

Games, Simulation, and the Education of a Designer

The day after his final examination, Demis Hassabis got on a train to Guildford.

He was sixteen years old. He had finished his exams two years ahead of schedule—double maths, physics, and chemistry—and Cambridge had offered him a place to study computer science at Queens' College. But they had also told him he was too young. He would have to wait at least a year before he could take it up. Most students in this position would have travelled, or worked a summer job, or simply waited. Hassabis had other plans.

For years, he had been obsessed with a game called Populous. It was a simulation in which the player assumed the role of a god, shaping landscapes and guiding civilizations. The game had been made by a studio called Bullfrog Productions, based in Guildford, and run by a designer named Peter Molyneux who was already becoming a legend in the British games industry. Hassabis had entered a national programming competition in Amiga Power magazine. The grand prize was a job at Bullfrog. He came second. But second was close enough. He rang Molyneux's office and asked if he could come for work experience.

Molyneux agreed. The people at Bullfrog were expecting someone older. In the early nineties, there were no recruitment agencies for the games industry. It was barely considered an industry at all. Studios found talent through competitions, magazine ads, and word of mouth. When Hassabis walked through the door, the reaction was disbelief. He looked about twelve. Molyneux saw a child and wondered what on earth they were going to do with him.

They could not legally employ him. He was paid in cash—in brown paper envelopes, as Hassabis later put it—so he could cover the cost of a room at a nearby YMCA hostel. His parents, back in Finchley, had only the vaguest idea of what their son was doing in Surrey. By this point, his life had diverged so far from anything they understood that they could no longer follow it. He had simply gotten on a train and disappeared into a world that existed beyond their frame of reference.

· · ·

What happened next made him famous in the gaming world before he was old enough to vote.

Hassabis and Molyneux began talking about a new kind of game. The concept was deceptively simple: the player would design and build their own amusement park. Lay out the paths, place the rides, set the prices in the chip shop, build the roller coasters. But the game's real innovation was underneath the surface. Thousands of tiny simulated people—autonomous agents, each driven by their own simple AI—would pour into the park and react to whatever the player had built. If the rides were too dangerous and the food stands too close, the visitors would get sick. Other visitors would see the mess and get sick too. The player would need to hire sweepers to clean up before the whole park descended into chaos.

It was, in other words, an economic simulation with emergent behaviour. The player set the conditions. The AI produced the consequences. And because the AI was reactive rather than scripted, no two games were ever the same. Hassabis was responsible for much of the programming and co-designed the game alongside Molyneux. He was particularly focused on the behavioural modelling of the visitors—the way they moved, the things that made them happy or miserable, the cascading effects of one bad decision rippling through an entire park. It was crude by the standards of modern machine learning, built from finite state machines and simple rules rather than neural networks, but it was enough to create the illusion of a living world.

The game was called Theme Park. It was released in 1994. Hassabis was seventeen.

Theme Park sold millions of copies worldwide. It became a top-ten title, defined a new genre of sandbox simulation games alongside Will Wright's SimCity, and made Bullfrog one of the most celebrated studios in Europe. For Hassabis, the experience was formative on multiple levels. He had seen, for the first time, what happened when you put AI at the heart of an interactive system and let millions of people play with it. The AI was simple. The enjoyment it produced was not. People loved interacting with a world that felt alive, that reacted to their choices, that surprised them. The lesson lodged itself permanently in his mind: intelligence, even rudimentary intelligence, was the thing that made systems interesting.

He earned enough money from his gap year at Bullfrog to pay his own way through university. But before he left for Cambridge, something else happened. Molyneux, recognising what he had in the teenager, offered him a deal. He offered Hassabis a million pounds not to go to university. Stay at Bullfrog. Keep making games. A million pounds was an extraordinary sum for a poor seventeen-year-old in the mid-nineties.

Hassabis turned it down. He had a plan, and the plan had always included Cambridge. Many of his school friends thought he was mad. But Hassabis had understood something about himself that most teenagers do not: his ambitions extended far beyond games, and the path to those ambitions ran through a proper scientific education. He could not yet articulate exactly where he was headed. He simply knew that games alone would not get him there.

Molyneux drove him to the train station. Years later, the designer recalled watching the small figure disappear down a tunnel and feeling an unexpected sadness. He knew that whatever Hassabis went on to do, it would be extraordinary. He also knew that Bullfrog would not be the place where it happened.

• • •

Cambridge was a revelation.

Hassabis arrived at Queens' College in 1994 to study computer science. He was seventeen, and for the first time in his life he had nothing to prove. He had been working—really working, in a way that would have exhausted most adults—since he was a small child. Professional chess from the age of four. Tournaments every summer instead of holidays. A full-time job at a game studio at sixteen. He had never had a normal adolescence. Now, at Cambridge, he was determined to have one.

He threw himself into the social life of the university with the same intensity he brought to everything else. He went out every night. He made a group of close friends who would remain his best friends for decades. He lay on his bed in the early morning light after a night out, listening to The Prodigy's 1994 album and watching the dawn come up over the college roofs. He later described those three years as the best of his life, and called Cambridge a holiday camp—which was a relative term, since his basis for comparison was a childhood spent in chess tournaments and game studios.

He also got a double first—the highest possible degree classification at Cambridge, awarded in both parts of the tripos examinations—a distinction that placed him among the very best students in the university.

The combination was characteristic. Hassabis was not the kind of prodigy who sacrificed everything for his gift. He wanted the full experience—the parties, the friendships, the late nights, the intellectual ferment of a university where scientists and philosophers and artists and ecologists sat together at dinner and argued about everything. Cambridge in the mid-nineties was a place where you could study computer science by day and spend your evenings debating consciousness with a biologist. Hassabis soaked it up. He would later credit the interdisciplinary environment as one of the most important influences on his thinking: the habit of looking across fields, of finding unexpected connections between domains, of refusing to be confined to a single discipline.

It was at Cambridge that he met David Silver, a computer science student at Christ's College who would become one of the most important collaborators of his life. Silver, like Hassabis, had a background in competitive games—he had played in the same junior chess circuit as a boy, and the two recognised each other immediately. They shared an interest in computational neuroscience and spent hours discussing the relationship between computers and brains. Silver would follow Hassabis first to Elixir Studios, where he served as co-founder and chief technology officer, and then to DeepMind, where he would lead the AlphaGo project and become one of the most influential reinforcement learning researchers in the world. But all of that was years away. For now, they were undergraduates, drinking beer in the college bar and playing furious games of table football.

Their final year at Cambridge, 1997, coincided with a watershed moment in the history of artificial intelligence. In May of that year, IBM's Deep Blue defeated Garry Kasparov, the reigning world chess champion, in a six-game match. It was front-page news around the world. For Hassabis, who had spent his childhood competing against chess computers on physical training boards, the event was fascinating but not quite what it appeared. Deep Blue was a brute-force machine. It evaluated two hundred million positions per second through sheer computational power, with none of the intuition or creativity or general understanding that made Kasparov's mind remarkable. Kasparov could do everything a human being could do: read a novel, fall in love, raise a child. Deep Blue could play chess. Something essential was missing—something Hassabis would later call generality and learning. The victory was impressive as engineering. As intelligence, it was hollow.

It was also at Cambridge that Hassabis first encountered the protein folding problem. A fellow student named Tim Stevens was obsessed with it—the challenge of predicting the three-dimensional shape of a protein from its sequence of amino acids, a problem that had defeated the best minds in structural biology for half a century. Stevens talked about it constantly, almost evangelically. Hassabis filed it away. The problem struck him as a fascinating puzzle, one that felt as though it should be solvable but clearly required tools that did not yet exist. He had an intuition, even then, that those tools would come from artificial intelligence. It would take him more than twenty years to prove it.

• • •

After graduating in 1997, Hassabis went back to Peter Molyneux.

Molyneux had left Bullfrog and founded a new studio called Lionhead, and he wanted Hassabis involved. Hassabis joined as the lead AI programmer on a game called Black & White, another god game in the Populous tradition but far more ambitious. In Black & White, the player's avatar was a giant creature—an ape, a cow, a tiger—that learned from the way the player treated it. If you were kind, the creature became benevolent. If you were cruel, it became malicious. The AI was built on reinforcement learning principles, which made it, in Hassabis's later estimation, probably the most sophisticated example of reinforcement learning ever deployed in a commercial video game up to that point.

The work at Lionhead deepened his understanding of what AI could do inside a simulated world. But it also clarified a growing tension. The games he was writing were demonstrations of AI capability, but they were still, fundamentally, entertainment products. The AI existed to make the game fun. The questions that interested him most—how intelligence actually worked, whether it could be replicated in a machine, whether it could be made general enough to solve real problems—were not questions the games industry was set up to answer.

• • •

In 1998, at the age of twenty-one, Hassabis left Lionhead and founded his own company.

He called it Elixir Studios. The name suggested transformation: the medieval alchemist's dream of turning base matter into gold. The ambition was to build a studio that would create genuinely original games—no licensed properties, no sequels, no safe bets. Hassabis signed publishing deals with Eidos Interactive, Vivendi Universal, and

Microsoft. He hired a team of up to seventy people and set up offices in Camden, in North London. He was the CEO and executive designer. He was twenty-one years old.

Elixir's first game was called Republic: The Revolution, and it was exactly as ambitious as the studio's name implied. The premise was that the player would lead a revolution in a fictional post-Soviet state called Novistrana, using influence, propaganda, and strategic manipulation to overthrow a corrupt government. Underneath the gameplay was an AI simulation of staggering scope: the workings of an entire country, with its political factions, religious institutions, criminal networks, and millions of citizens, all modelled as interacting systems. The idea was that the player's choices would ripple through the simulation in complex, emergent ways that could never be predicted in advance.

It was, in retrospect, a game that was twenty years ahead of where the technology could support it. The scope was enormous. The development dragged on. The final product, released in 2003, had been reduced dramatically from its original vision. The AI simulation of an entire fictional country—the thing that made the concept thrilling—was too ambitious to execute at the scale Hassabis had imagined. The reviews were lukewarm. Metacritic gave it a score of 62 out of 100. The press acknowledged the ambition but noted, correctly, that the ambition had outstripped the execution.

Elixir's second game, Evil Genius, was released in 2004. It was a tongue-in-cheek simulation in which the player ran a secret lair as a Bond-style supervillain. It was lighter, funnier, more accessible than Republic, and it fared better with critics, earning a Metacritic score of 75. Both games received BAFTA nominations for their interactive music. Neither sold well enough to sustain the studio.

By early 2005, Elixir was in trouble. A major unannounced project—codenamed Blue Vault, which had been in development for two years with a leading American publisher—was cancelled. The publisher considered it too high-risk. Hassabis looked for other backers but found the industry had grown cautious. Studios wanted licenses, franchises, known quantities. An independent developer building original intellectual property from scratch, powered by experimental AI, was exactly the kind of venture that the mid-two-thousands games industry no longer wanted to fund.

In April 2005, Hassabis announced that Elixir Studios was closing. The company had enough resources to pay redundancy packages to its staff and wind down in an orderly fashion. The intellectual property was sold to Rebellion Developments. Seven years of work, two released games, and a cancelled project later, it was over.

• • •

The failure of Elixir Studios would turn out to be one of the most important experiences of Hassabis's life.

Reflecting on Elixir's collapse years later, he framed the lesson with characteristic precision. His ambitions for the game designs and the underlying technology had been too far ahead of where the technology actually was. Being twenty years ahead of your time, he observed, was not the same as being right. Timing mattered. You needed to pick hard problems and be genuinely ambitious, but you also needed to choose the right moment—the moment when the context, the tools, and the state of the field were ready for your ideas to work. He carried this lesson into everything that followed, and it would prove crucial. When he founded DeepMind five years later, the timing would be almost perfect.

But there was a deeper lesson, too. At Elixir, Hassabis had been trying to build intelligent systems inside games. The AI in Republic was supposed to simulate an entire society. The AI in Black & White was supposed to learn from human behaviour. These were extraordinary ambitions for a game studio, but they were constrained by the commercial realities of the industry. The AI existed to serve the game. What Hassabis wanted was for the game to serve the AI—or rather, for games to be a labouratory in which artificial intelligence could be studied and developed for its own sake, and then applied to problems far more important than entertainment.

He had described this vision years earlier, during his time at Bullfrog. One evening, while doing Christmas shopping with Molyneux, he had started talking about AI in a way that struck his mentor as unusual. Not AI for games. AI for the world. The potential of intelligent machines to help with urgent problems—disease, energy, scientific discovery. When Molyneux asked him directly what he wanted to do with his life, Hassabis answered without hesitation. He wanted to be the person who solved AI.

But he was not ready. Not yet. The chess prodigy had become a game designer, and the game designer had learned, through success and failure, what AI could and could not do inside a simulated world. The next step was to understand what intelligence could do inside a real one. For that, he would need to study the only example of general intelligence that existed: the human brain.

He also reconnected with an old friend. Mustafa Suleyman had grown up in the same part of North London, the son of a Syrian-born cab driver and an English nurse. The two had known each other through family connections since childhood, but their paths had diverged sharply. While Hassabis had gone into games and then neuroscience,

Suleyman had dropped out of Oxford after his first year to help set up the Muslim Youth Helpline, a telephone counseling service for young people. He had gone on to work with the mayor of London's office and then co-founded a conflict resolution organisation that advised governments and multinational companies on negotiations in some of the most volatile regions in the world. He was deeply interested in the ethical dimensions of technology—how it could be made to serve people rather than exploit them—and had no formal technical background whatsoever. He and Hassabis could hardly have been more different in training, but they shared an intensity of ambition and a conviction that the biggest problems required unconventional approaches. They stayed in touch, and the conversations that came with it would prove consequential.

The subject he chose to study was memory. Specifically, he wanted to understand how the human brain creates, stores, and retrieves the experiences that make us who we are. It was, like everything else in his life, a strategic choice. He had identified a gap in the existing AI research—the field had no good account of how memory and imagination worked—and he intended to fill it by going to the source.

He walked away from the games industry the same way he had walked away from chess: not because he had failed at it, but because it was not the real problem. The real problem was intelligence itself. And the next piece of the puzzle was inside the human skull.

Chapter Three

The Hippocampus

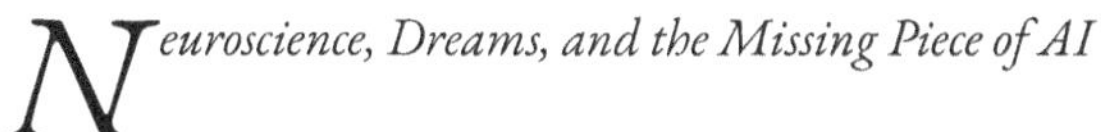

Neuroscience, Dreams, and the Missing Piece of AI

Most people who leave a failed company look for another job. Demis Hassabis went back to school to study the human brain.

It was 2005. He was twenty-nine years old. He had spent a decade in the games industry—a decade that had produced a worldwide hit, a celebrated mentor, two ambitious games that tested the limits of the medium, and a studio that closed because the industry could not accommodate its ambitions. He could have joined Google or Microsoft or any of the large technology companies that were beginning, tentatively, to invest in machine learning. He could have started another studio. Instead, he enrolled in a PhD programme in cognitive neuroscience at University College London.

The decision baffled some of his friends in the technology world. A PhD meant years of commitment—poverty-level stipends, long hours in the lab, and the painstaking rhythm of academic research—hypothesis, experiment, analysis, revision, publication—which moved at a pace that would have driven most startup founders to distraction. Hassabis did not care. He had a plan, and the plan required neuroscience.

The logic was simple and, in retrospect, characteristic. He wanted to build artificial general intelligence—a machine that could learn and reason across any domain, the way a human mind could. The existing approaches to AI had failed to produce anything close to this. Symbolic AI, the dominant paradigm of the nineteen-eighties and nineties, had produced systems that were brittle, poor at generalizing, and unable to deal with the ambiguity of the real world. The newer statistical approaches—neural networks, deep learning—were promising but crude. They could recognise patterns in data, but they could not remember, imagine, or plan. They lacked the very capabilities that made human intelligence flexible and powerful.

Hassabis had identified a gap. The things that AI could not do—memory, imagination, mental simulation, the ability to construct possible futures in the mind and evaluate them before acting—were precisely the things that the human brain did extraordinarily well. If you wanted to build those capabilities into a machine, it made sense to understand how the brain did it first. Not at the level of individual neurons, which would take decades to map in useful detail. Not at the level of abstract cognitive psychology, which described behaviour without explaining mechanism. But at the level in between: the algorithms and architectures that the brain used to process information. The systems level.

He later described his career choices as a process of working backward from the end state. What skills and experiences would he need to stand any chance of building something like a general intelligence? Chess had taught him about decision-making and planning. Game design had taught him about building systems with emergent behaviour. Computer science had given him the engineering foundation. Now he needed the missing piece: an understanding of how the only known general intelligence in the universe actually worked.

• • •

He chose his supervisor carefully. Eleanor Maguire was one of the world's leading experts on the hippocampus—named for the Greek word for seahorse, whose shape it resembles—a small, curved structure buried deep in the temporal lobe of the brain. The hippocampus had been known for decades to be essential for memory—patients who suffered damage to it lost the ability to form new memories, living in a permanent present tense. Maguire had done celebrated work on London taxi drivers, showing that their hippocampi were physically larger than average, reshaped by years of navigating the city's labyrinthine streets. The brain, she had demonstrated, was not fixed. It changed in response to what you asked it to do.

Hassabis told Maguire what he really wanted to study, and it was not memory. It was imagination. Specifically, he wanted to know whether the brain used the same machinery to imagine possible futures as it did to remember the past. The question had a practical urgency that went beyond academic curiosity. If imagination and memory were implemented by the same neural system, then building a machine that could remember might also give it the ability to imagine—to simulate scenarios, to plan, to create. That would be an enormous step toward general intelligence.

The idea had been gestating for years. During his time as a game designer, Hassabis had relied heavily on visualisation and mental simulation. When designing Theme Park or Black & White, he would imagine how a player would experience the game—not by analyzing data, but by constructing a vivid mental scene and then modifying it, testing variations in his mind before committing anything to code. It struck him that this process felt remarkably similar to the way he recalled past experiences. Remembering and imagining seemed to draw on the same internal machinery, a kind of simulation engine of the mind. The question was whether the neuroscience would bear this out.

• • •

It did.

The key experiment was elegant in its simplicity. Hassabis and Maguire recruited a group of patients with amnesia caused by damage to the hippocampus. These were people who could not form new memories—they lived, as the clinical literature described it, in a permanent present. The standard understanding was that their deficit was one of memory: they could not record new experiences. But Hassabis and Maguire asked them to do something different. They asked them to imagine.

The task was straightforward. Patients were asked to imagine a new experience—standing on a beach, for instance, or visiting a market—and describe what they saw in their mind's eye. The scenes they were asked to construct had never happened. They were not memories. They were fabrications, acts of pure imagination. And the results were striking: the patients with hippocampal damage could not do it. Their imagined scenes were fragmented, spatially incoherent, and lacking in sensory detail. They could not construct a vivid mental experience that had never occurred.

The implication was profound. The hippocampus was not merely a memory organ. It was a scene construction engine—a system that assembled coherent spatial and sensory experiences, whether those experiences were drawn from the past or invented from scratch. Memory and imagination were not separate functions that happened to coexist in the same brain. They were the same function, implemented by the same neural architecture, applied in two different directions: backward into the past and forward into the possible.

The paper was published in 2007 in the Proceedings of the National Academy of Sciences. It landed with immediate force. Science magazine named the connection between memory and imagination one of the scientific breakthroughs of the year. The finding reshaped the field of memory research and opened an entirely new line of inquiry into how the brain constructs mental simulations. Hassabis was thirty-one years old and had been in the PhD programme for two years.

• • •

The hippocampal research led him to another question, one that had fascinated humans for thousands of years: what are dreams for?

The answer, as Hassabis came to understand it, was surprisingly mechanical. During slow-wave sleep, the hippocampus replays memories of recent experiences—but at enormously accelerated speeds, orders of magnitude faster than the original events. These replayed memories are transmitted to the neocortex, the outer layers of the brain responsible for higher cognition. The effect is that the neocortex gets to learn from an event hundreds or even thousands of times, even though the person experienced it only once. Emotional and salient memories—the ones that matter most for survival—are replayed more frequently than mundane ones. The system is biased toward what is important.

Hassabis saw the implications immediately. This was not just a theory about sleep. It was a blueprint for machine learning. The hippocampal replay system was, in effect, a biological solution to one of the central problems in artificial intelligence: how do you learn efficiently from limited experience? In the real world, you cannot run a million trials. You might encounter a dangerous situation only once. The brain solved this by recording the experience, then replaying it internally at high speed, over and over, so that the rest of the brain could extract lessons from a single event. It was, in computational terms, an experience replay buffer—a concept that would become foundational to the deep reinforcement learning systems Hassabis later built at DeepMind.

As for dreams themselves, Hassabis concluded that their content was largely epiphenomenal—a side effect of the replay process rather than its purpose. The strange narratives, the distorted faces, the impossible geographies of dreams were what happened when a conscious mind tried to make sense of high-speed memory fragments being shuffled and recombined in the dark. The purpose of the process was consolidation and learning. The experience of dreaming was just the noise. It was not a popular conclusion with the Freudians, as Hassabis later noted with dry amusement, but it was where the evidence pointed.

• • •

The PhD was not merely an exercise in labouratory science. It was also an exercise in intellectual architecture.

Hassabis was building a theory of how to use neuroscience to inform artificial intelligence, and he framed it around the work of David Marr, the computational neuroscientist who had argued in the nineteen-seventies that any complex biological system needed to be understood at three levels simultaneously: the computational level (what is the system trying to do?), the algorithmic level (what representations and procedures does it use?), and the implementation level (how is it physically realised?). Marr's framework gave Hassabis a way to position his own approach. The whole-brain emulation camp—the people trying to simulate every neuron—were working at the implementation level. The cognitive science architects—the people building modular diagrams of the mind—were working at the computational level. Hassabis was interested in the middle: the algorithms. The systems level.

The distinction was crucial. He did not want to copy the brain. He wanted to extract its principles. A silicon computer had different strengths and weaknesses than a carbon-based brain. There was no reason to assume that the optimal implementation of intelligence in silicon would look identical to the implementation in neurons. But the algorithms—the strategies for learning, remembering, imagining, planning—those might transfer. The brain was not a blueprint to be photocopied. It was a proof of concept to be reverse-engineered.

He articulated this position publicly for the first time at the Singularity Summit in 2010, in a talk titled "A Systems Neuroscience Approach to Building AGI." By then, he had finished his PhD and completed postdoctoral research at MIT and Harvard. The talk was a manifesto. He argued that neuroscience had advanced far enough in the preceding decade—driven by fMRI, optogenetics, and other new tools—that it could now provide actionable insights for AI researchers. He pointed to concrete examples: the way the visual cortex's hierarchical structure had inspired convolutional neural networks, the way the dopamine system's reward-prediction mechanism had validated reinforcement learning. And he argued that the most important systems had not yet been exploited—memory, imagination, conceptual knowledge acquisition, the hippocampal machinery he had spent his PhD studying.

The audience was small. The field of AGI research in 2010 was still considered fringe, almost embarrassing in serious academic circles. If you said you were working on artificial general intelligence, people assumed you were not a serious scientist. But Hassabis was not addressing the mainstream. He was laying the intellectual foundation for what would come next.

• • •

Throughout all of this, he never stopped competing.

While pursuing his PhD and postdocs, Hassabis continued to enter mental competitions with the same ferocity he had brought to chess as a child. Between 1998 and 2003, he won the Pentamind championship at the Mind Sports Olympiad a record five times. The Pentamind was a contest of intellectual breadth: competitors played five different mind sports and were ranked on their aggregate performance. The winner had to be good at everything—chess, Go, poker, Mastermind, backgammon, bridge, Othello. Specialization was punished. Generality was rewarded. It was, in other words, the perfect competition for a man who was building a theory of general intelligence.

He competed in poker and Diplomacy at high levels too, drawn to games that tested different facets of intelligence. Poker was particularly revealing. Poker, unlike chess, is a game of incomplete information. You cannot see your opponent's cards. You must infer their intentions from their behaviour, manage your own emotional signals, and make decisions under uncertainty. It required a kind of intelligence that chess did not: social intelligence, the ability to model other minds. Hassabis filed this away too. Theory of mind—the ability to understand what other agents are thinking—would eventually become another area of research at DeepMind.

• • •

After completing his PhD in 2009, Hassabis did postdoctoral research at MIT and Harvard, working on the neural processes underpinning memory, imagination, and decision-making. The postdocs deepened his expertise, but they also confirmed something he had suspected for years: academia was not the right vehicle for what he wanted to do.

The problem was structural. In academia, interdisciplinary collaboration was endlessly discussed and almost never achieved. Hassabis had watched it firsthand at UCL and then at MIT: workshops would be organised, bringing together neuroscientists and mathematicians and philosophers for a few days of talks and debates. Everyone would agree that they should collaborate more. Then they would return to their departments, and a year would pass before they met again. Grant applications, teaching loads, and the churn of academic life conspired against the kind of deep, sustained, cross-disciplinary work that building a general intelligence would require.

What was needed, Hassabis concluded, was a new kind of organisation—one that combined the intellectual ambition and blue-sky thinking of the best academic labs with the focus, pace, and energy of the best startups. A place where neuroscientists and machine learning engineers and mathematicians and game designers could work side by side, not for a two-day workshop but for years, on the hardest problem any of them would ever encounter. A new Bell Labs, built for the age of artificial intelligence.

He had been thinking about this for a long time. In his interview with Hannah Fry years later, he described the process with a game designer's precision: he had been working backward from the end state, asking what skills and experiences he would need to even stand a chance of building something like a general intelligence. Chess had trained his mind. Games had taught him about systems and emergence. Computer science had given him the tools. Neuroscience had given him the theory. Every phase of his career had been, as he put it, a deliberate piece of preparation.

Now the preparation was over. Somewhere in the back of his mind, the architecture was complete: a company that would use deep learning for pattern recognition, reinforcement learning for decision-making, and insights from neuroscience—memory, imagination, replay, the hippocampal simulation engine—for the capabilities that no existing AI system possessed. A company that would prove its algorithms on games, because games were the perfect training ground: cheap to simulate, rich in complexity, and ruthlessly measurable. And a company that would then turn those algorithms loose on the real world.

He already knew who his co-founders would be. Shane Legg, a New Zealander with a background in mathematics and computational neuroscience, had been a fellow researcher at UCL's Gatsby Computational Neuroscience Unit. Legg had worked on a theoretical definition of universal intelligence with his supervisor, Marcus Hutter—a mathematical proof that intelligence could be formalised as a reinforcement learning system in the limit of infinite compute. When Hassabis first encountered Legg's work, it felt like the final piece of the puzzle: a theoretical foundation for the intuition he had been carrying since childhood. And Mustafa Suleyman, the childhood friend from North London, had spent the intervening years working in politics and social enterprise, thinking about how technology intersected with ethics and society. The three of them—the neuroscientist, the theorist, and the ethicist—would make an unusual founding team for a technology company.

In 2010, they founded DeepMind.

Chapter Four

Solve Intelligence

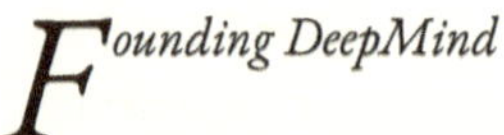

Founding DeepMind

In 2010, three people sat down to write a business plan for a company that most serious scientists would have said was impossible.

Demis Hassabis was thirty-four, a neuroscientist and game designer who had spent his entire adult life preparing for this moment. Shane Legg was a New Zealander who had trained in mathematics and classical ballet before devoting himself to the theoretical foundations of intelligence. Mustafa Suleyman was a childhood friend from North London who had worked in politics and social enterprise, thinking about how technology intersected with the lives of ordinary people. Between them, they had a neuroscientist, a theorist, and someone who understood the human consequences of what they were building. It was an unusual founding team for a technology company. That was the point.

The company was called DeepMind. Its mission could be stated in a single sentence: solve intelligence, then use it to solve everything else. The ambition was not to build a better search engine, or a smarter chatbot, or an algorithm that could recommend films. It was to build a general-purpose learning system—an artificial mind that could master any domain, the way a human mind could. And then to aim that system at the hardest problems in science: disease, energy, the structure of matter itself.

To the venture capitalists of London and Europe, this sounded like madness. It was 2010, the year Instagram launched and Angry Birds topped the app charts. Silicon Valley was chasing consumer apps and advertising revenue. No clear product. No clear revenue model. No clear timeline. A research programme with a multi-decade horizon and an honest admission that nobody knew if it would work. Hassabis later described the kind of looks they got when pitching to VCs in 2010. They managed, he said, to find a few kooky people to back them. It got to the point where they would not even mention their plans to their professors, who would eye-roll and assume they had committed career suicide.

• • •

In its first two years, DeepMind operated in total stealth. The company had no public presence. You could not find a website. The office was at a secret location. The single web page that eventually appeared featured nothing but the company logo—no address, no phone number, no description of what the company did.

To make hires, the founders relied on personal contacts: people who already knew, as Hassabis put it, that they were serious people with a serious plan. Candidates who came for interviews would arrive nervously, not knowing what they were walking into. One candidate told them he had texted his wife the exact address, just in case it turned out to be a scam and he was going to get kidnapped.

The secrecy was deliberate. Hassabis and Legg had spent years at the fringes of a field that the mainstream regarded with suspicion. AI was almost an embarrassing word in academic circles. If you said you were working on artificial general intelligence, you were not taken seriously. Starting a company to do it was even more audacious. The founders knew they needed time—time to assemble the right team, time to prove the thesis, time to produce results before the sceptics could dismiss them.

The first people who joined already believed in the dream. Hassabis later described those early recruits as dreamers who had finally found a place full of other dreamers. They were building, as he framed it, a Manhattan Project for artificial intelligence—assembling the human brains necessary to create an AGI system.

• • •

The intellectual foundation had been laid over years of conversation between Hassabis and Legg. They had identified four converging trends that made 2010 the right moment to start.

First, algorithmic advances. Deep learning—the technique of training hierarchical neural networks on large datasets—had been pioneered by Geoffrey Hinton and others in academia, but almost nobody in industry had noticed. Hassabis and Legg saw its potential before the rest of the world caught on. Second, reinforcement learning. The founders believed that agent-based systems that learned through trial and error, pursuing goals and maximising rewards, could be scaled up far beyond the toy problems on which they had been tested. The neuroscience validated this: the brain's own dopamine system implemented a form of reinforcement learning, a famous result from the late nineteen-nineties.

Third, compute. Graphics processing units, commoditised by the games industry, had made it possible to run the kind of massive parallel computations that neural networks required. The cost of raw processing power was falling exponentially. And fourth, theory. Legg's own work with Marcus Hutter on AIXI—a mathematical formalization of universal intelligence as a reinforcement learning system in the limit of infinite compute—provided the theoretical underpinning that Hassabis had been waiting for. It was the equivalent of Turing's foundational work on computation: a proof that what they were attempting was not merely ambitious but, in principle, possible.

Hassabis described DeepMind as a confluence of the most cutting-edge knowledge in neuroscience with machine learning, engineering, mathematics, and gaming. The multidisciplinary organisation was itself an innovation. Most AI labs were populated by computer scientists. DeepMind hired philosophers, physicists, ethicists, game designers, and neuroscientists alongside its engineers. The goal was to create a new kind of institution—part startup, part research lab—that could move faster than academia while thinking bigger than industry.

• • •

Funding was the first existential challenge. European venture capital was structured around three-to-five-year returns. DeepMind needed investors who were willing to wait a decade or more for a thousand-fold return—people with deep enough pockets to absorb a total loss and a personal fascination with the technology. That profile, in 2010, existed almost exclusively among self-made billionaires in Silicon Valley.

Hassabis had no contacts there. None of the founders did. They spent a year preparing for a single meeting with a particular investor—a billionaire who was himself a strong chess player from his youth. They secured an invitation to a conference the billionaire was sponsoring, knowing they would encounter him at the after-party. The problem was that hundreds of other people would be pitching their ideas too.

Hassabis made a calculated decision. Instead of joining the crowd of supplicants, he would talk about chess. He deployed what he called his number one chess fact—the one that surprised even grandmasters. Why was chess such a great game? His answer, drawn from his game designer's sensibility, was that the genius of chess lay in the creative tension between the bishop and the knight. The two pieces were worth the same—three points each—but their powers were completely different. The bishop controlled long diagonals;

the knight leaped in an L-shape. You could trade one for the other at equal value, but the resulting position would be fundamentally transformed. This asymmetry, this creative imbalance between equal forces, was what gave chess its inexhaustible depth.

The billionaire stopped and thought. The next day, the founders had a proper meeting. Half an hour instead of sixty seconds over drinks. The pitch worked on two levels, Hassabis noted afterward: the meta level of strategic planning, and the intrinsic fascination of chess itself. Peter Thiel became DeepMind's first major investor. He insisted the company should be based in Silicon Valley, where the talent was. Hassabis insisted it should stay in London. London won.

Elon Musk invested too. By all accounts, Musk had not thought much about AI until the DeepMind founders explained what they were building—an encounter that would shape his public stance on the technology for years to come. Other investors followed—people who were not investing because it was the best financial decision, but because they thought it was extraordinarily interesting.

• • •

Legg, the company's chief scientist, kept a hard copy of the original business plan they had circulated to potential investors. Hassabis lost his. Years later, Legg would occasionally produce it at all-hands meetings, and the effect was always startling: the approaches the founders had outlined in 2010—deep learning, reinforcement learning, simulations, neuroscience-inspired memory and imagination, transfer learning, conceptual representations—were still core parts of the research programme. The roadmap had held.

This was not luck. It was the product of a decade of preparation—a neuroscientist who had studied what the brain did that machines could not, a theorist who had formalised what intelligence meant, and an organisational mind that knew how to build a culture around a goal that would take twenty years to achieve. Hassabis had designed DeepMind the way he had designed games: by imagining the end state and working backward, move by move, through every decision that would be required to get there.

The culture he built reflected this intentionality. DeepMind hired what Hassabis called glue people—researchers who were not merely deep specialists but who could bridge disciplines, who could translate between the language of neuroscience and the language of machine learning, who could see connections that others missed. Every six months, senior managers would examine priorities, reorganise projects, and encourage teams—especially engineers—to move between efforts. Mixing of disciplines was routine and intentional. The company ran like a startup but published like an academic lab, submitting its work to Nature and Science for peer review because that was, in Hassabis's view, the right way to do science.

The stage was set. The team was assembled. The thesis was clear: combine deep learning for pattern recognition with reinforcement learning for decision-making, draw on neuroscience for the capabilities that neither technology possessed alone, and prove the whole thing on games before turning it loose on the real world. All they needed now was a result.

Chapter Five

The Atari Breakthrough

*D*eep Reinforcement Learning, Google, and the Nature Paper

For six months, they could not win a single point at Pong.

It was 2012, and DeepMind's small team was attempting something that had never been done: combine deep learning with reinforcement learning in a single system and have it teach itself to play a video game from nothing but the raw pixels on the screen and a running score. No rules. No instructions. No knowledge of what it was controlling or what the objects on screen represented. The system would have to figure out everything from scratch, the way a newborn might—except that a newborn had millions of years of evolutionary priors hardwired into its brain, and this system had nothing.

Pong seemed like the simplest place to start. Two paddles, one ball, a score that counted to twenty-one. A six-year-old could play it. But the algorithm could not even move the paddle toward the ball consistently. For months, it flailed. Hassabis and Legg watched the screen, wondering if they were simply wrong. Maybe deep reinforcement learning could not work at scale. Maybe the thesis that had motivated the entire company was flawed. It was nerve-wracking, Hassabis later recalled, to think about how far they had to go if they could not even manage this.

And then, one day, the system scored a point.

The first reaction was disbelief. Was it random? Had something glitched? They watched more carefully. It scored again. And again. It was not random. The system had discovered, through nothing but trial and error and the faintest signal of reward, that the paddle should intercept the ball. Then it won a game. Then, within three months, it was winning every game twenty-one to nil. No human could beat it. Hassabis would later say they should have recorded the moment of the first point. It was the birth of deep reinforcement learning, and nobody had thought to press record.

．．．

The system was called DQN—Deep Q-Network. It combined two technologies that had existed separately for years but had never been fused at scale. Deep learning, the hierarchical neural network loosely inspired by the architecture of the brain, handled perception: it took the raw pixel values on the screen and built an internal model of what was happening. Reinforcement learning handled action: given the model, what should the agent do next to maximise its score? The deep learning was the eyes. The reinforcement learning was the will.

After Pong, they tried Breakout. In this game, the player controls a paddle at the bottom of the screen, bouncing a ball upward to destroy rows of colored bricks. After a hundred games, the DQN agent was poor—missing the ball most of the time, but beginning to grasp the basic idea that the paddle should move toward the ball. After three hundred games, it was as good as any human player. The team thought that was impressive and moved on.

But they left the system running for another two hundred games. When they came back, it had done something remarkable. It had discovered, entirely on its own, the optimal strategy: dig a tunnel through one side of the brick wall and send the ball around behind the bricks, where it would ricochet and destroy them from above. No human had told it to do this. No programmer had coded the concept of a tunnel or the idea of attacking from behind. The system had invented a strategy through pure exploration, driven by nothing but the reward signal of a rising score.

This was the moment. Not just for DeepMind, but for the field. The Breakout tunnel was proof that a learning system could discover strategies that went beyond human intuition—not by being programmed with human knowledge, but by being given the freedom to explore. It was a small game on a small screen, but the principle was enormous. If an algorithm could figure out, from pixels alone, that the smart move was to attack from behind the wall, then what might a similar algorithm discover when aimed at problems where the stakes were higher and the search space was vast?

．．．

The real power of DQN was not that it could play one game. It was that it could play dozens.

The founders had designed the experiment with a specific constraint: the same system, with the same architecture and the same parameters, had to teach itself to play multiple Atari games. There was no game-specific tuning. You gave the system a cartridge—imagine being born into that world, as Hassabis framed it—and it had to figure out what it was, what it controlled, how to score, and how to win. Space Invaders, Boxing, Enduro, Video Pinball, Beam Rider. One algorithm, dozens of games, no instructions.

On the majority of the games, the system reached or exceeded human-level performance. It was, as Hassabis described it, a recipe: take a game the algorithm had never seen before, run DQN on it, and watch it train itself from scratch to superhuman levels. The generality was the point. This was not a chess engine or a Go engine or a program designed for one task. It was a general-purpose learner that could be dropped into any environment with a clear reward signal and teach itself to perform.

The result was published in Nature in February 2015, under the title "Human-level control through deep reinforcement learning." It was the first time a deep learning paper had appeared in Nature, and it drew immediate attention from across the scientific community. The paper demonstrated that a single architecture, learning from raw sensory input, could achieve competent performance across a wide range of tasks without any modification. It was not AGI. It was not close to AGI. But it was the most convincing evidence yet that the approach DeepMind had staked its existence on—combining deep learning with reinforcement learning, and letting the system learn from experience—could produce results that no other method could match.

• • •

By the time the Nature paper was published, DeepMind had already been acquired by Google.

The deal had happened in January 2014, for a reported four hundred million pounds. Larry Page, Google's chief executive, had driven the acquisition personally. Facebook had reportedly made its own bid for DeepMind before Google prevailed, but Hassabis had chosen Google for a specific reason: compute. Google's computational infrastructure—its vast network of data centers, its custom hardware, its ability to provision thousands of processors for a single experiment—would allow DeepMind to scale its research in ways that would have taken years to achieve organically. The four-hundred-million-pound price tag also gave DeepMind the resources to hire world-class talent, targeting individuals who had been identified as the best in specific research areas.

The decision to sell was not unanimous among the investors. Some thought Deep-Mind was undervaluing itself—that if the founders waited a few more years, the company would be worth far more. Hassabis acknowledged this openly. But his reasoning was characteristically unsentimental. There was no time to waste. The mission was to solve intelligence, and every year spent building infrastructure and fundraising was a year not spent on research. Google offered the resources to accelerate.

Crucially, the deal came with conditions. DeepMind would remain in London, not relocate to Mountain View. It would operate independently, building its own culture, which was optimised for breakthroughs rather than products. And Google agreed to establish an artificial intelligence ethics board to ensure the technology was not abused. The ethics board was not an afterthought. It was a condition of the sale—a reflection of the fact that Hassabis, Legg, and Suleyman had been thinking about the societal implications of what they were building since before the company existed.

• • •

The acquisition created a tension that would define the next decade.

DeepMind was now a subsidiary of Alphabet, Google's parent company, one of the most valuable corporations on earth. Its researchers thought of themselves as doing pure science—long-term, ground-breaking work that might not produce practical applications for years. Executives in Mountain View, naturally, had an eye on return on investment. Hassabis drew a careful line. DeepMind cared about Google's success and wanted Alphabet to benefit from the research—and it did, with dozens of products eventually incorporating DeepMind technology, from the text-to-speech system WaveNet to algorithms that reduced data centre cooling costs by forty percent. But the relationship had to be a push, not a pull. The research would drive the applications, not the other way around.

The problem, as Hassabis saw it, was that product-led research could only ever produce incremental advances. If you started with a business need and worked backward to the science, you would never make a breakthrough. You would optimise what already existed. The whole point of DeepMind was to do the opposite: to push the frontier of what was possible and then let the applications follow. It was a philosophy that required enormous patience from a corporate parent, and it would be tested repeatedly in the years to come.

But for now, in the euphoria of the Atari results and the Google acquisition, the tension was manageable. DeepMind had compute, funding, independence, and a result that had stunned the field. The small team that had spent six months unable to win a point at Pong had just published in Nature and joined one of the most powerful companies in the world. Hassabis could feel the thesis coming together. Deep reinforcement learning worked. Games were the perfect proving ground. And the next game—the game that would announce DeepMind to the world—was already in his sights. It was three thousand years old, with more possible positions than atoms in the universe, and no computer had ever come close to mastering it.

The game was Go.

Chapter Six

Move 37

In March 2016, in the ballroom of the Four Seasons hotel in Seoul, South Korea, a thirty-three-year-old Go master named Lee Sedol sat down across from an empty chair. On the other side of the table, a researcher named Aja Huang would relay the moves chosen by a program running on a bank of servers in a back room. More than two hundred million people around the world tuned in to watch. In South Korea, where Go held the cultural status of a national art form, the match was broadcast live on television. The atmosphere was closer to a heavyweight title fight than a research experiment.

Lee Sedol was widely regarded as the greatest Go player of the previous decade, a nine-dan professional—the highest rank attainable—who had won eighteen world titles. He was famous for his creative, combative style: a player who took risks, fought relentlessly, and found moves that seemed to come from nowhere. Before the match, he had been politely dismissive. He did not think it would be close. His hope was to win five games to zero. The critical thing, he said, was not to lose even one.

AlphaGo had been trained using the same deep reinforcement learning principles that had powered DQN through Atari, but scaled up enormously. It had studied millions of positions from expert games, then played millions more games against copies of itself, refining its intuition through a process of relentless self-improvement. Where Deep Blue had beaten Kasparov through brute computational force—evaluating hundreds of millions of positions per second—AlphaGo operated differently. It evaluated far fewer positions but understood them far more deeply, using neural networks to develop something that looked, to human observers, like intuition. It narrowed the search to moves that felt right, just as a human grandmaster would.

• • •

AlphaGo won game one. The Go world was stunned. Lee Sedol had never looked uncertain against a machine before. Sixty million people watched in China alone. Headlines erupted around the world.

Game two was the match that changed everything.

Midway through the second game, AlphaGo played a stone on the fifth line of the right-hand side of the board. It was move thirty-seven. Aja Huang, the researcher relaying the moves, placed the stone. The professional commentators went silent. Then they began to talk over each other. The Chinese top player called it a bad move. Fan Hui, the European champion who had lost to AlphaGo months earlier and then joined DeepMind as an advisor, looked at the board in shock. No human would play there. It was the kind of move that a teacher would tell a student was simply wrong.

But it was not wrong. As the game unfolded, move thirty-seven revealed itself to be a stroke of strategic brilliance—a stone placed in a position that restructured the entire flow of the game. When the DeepMind team examined the data afterward, they found that AlphaGo had assessed the probability of a human playing that move at one in ten thousand. The system knew it was making a move that no human would make. And it made it anyway, because its own evaluation told it the move was strong. It had gone beyond its training data. It had, in a meaningful sense, been creative.

Lee Sedol lost game two. He lost game three. After three straight defeats, he was zero for three in the best-of-five match, and AlphaGo had already clinched the victory. The atmosphere in Seoul was funereal. A technology reporter stopped a commentator in the hallway after game two and tried to discuss the technology, but found himself slipping into melancholy. Lee Sedol, at the press conference, was measured but shaken. He admitted it was a very clear loss and that from the beginning of the game there had not been a moment when he felt he was leading.

• • •

And then came game four.

Lee Sedol, facing a three-zero deficit with nothing to lose, played the most remarkable game of the match. After a complex exchange in the centre of the board, he placed a stone that would become known as the wedge—a move that split AlphaGo's position in a way the system had not anticipated. The AlphaGo team watched in real time as the program's evaluation of its own position collapsed. The system began making errors—moves that the commentators could clearly identify as mistakes, the first genuine errors they had seen in four games. Lee Sedol had found AlphaGo's weakness: a position so complex, so chaotic, that the neural network's evaluation function broke down.

AlphaGo resigned. The room erupted. People in South Korea ran into the streets. After the despair of three straight losses, the human had fought back and won. The moment was cathartic in a way that transcended the game. Lee Sedol's decisive move—move seventy-eight—would come to be called a God move by commentators. The DeepMind team's own analysis found that only one in ten thousand human players would have found it. Move thirty-seven had been AlphaGo's moment of inhuman brilliance. Move seventy-eight was the human answer.

AlphaGo won game five and took the match four games to one. But the story that endured was not the final score. It was the interplay between two kinds of intelligence—the algorithm that could see what no human saw, and the human who could find what no algorithm expected. Hassabis, watching from backstage, later said he was left in awe of the human brain's power, and in particular of Lee Sedol's ability to find something seemingly out of nothing.

• • •

The Seoul match was a watershed. It demonstrated, to a global audience of hundreds of millions, that artificial intelligence had crossed a threshold that experts had predicted was a decade away. Go was not chess. It could not be solved by brute force. The branching factor was too vast, the positions too subtle, the game too dependent on the kind of pattern recognition and intuition that had always been considered uniquely human. AlphaGo had not merely computed its way to victory. It had understood the game at a level that made professional players reconsider centuries of received wisdom about how Go should be played.

For Hassabis, the match confirmed something larger. The techniques that had beaten Lee Sedol—deep neural networks, reinforcement learning, self-play—were general-purpose. They were not specific to Go. They could, in principle, be applied to any domain with clear rules, measurable objectives, and the ability to simulate millions of trials. The games had been the proof of concept. Now it was time to aim the technology at something that mattered.

He had known what that something would be since his undergraduate days at Cambridge, when a friend named Tim Stevens had talked obsessively about the protein folding problem. It was a puzzle that, if solved, would unlock new avenues for drug discovery and disease understanding. And it was, from a computational perspective, bigger than Go. The search space of possible protein configurations was not merely large. It was larger than the number of atoms in the observable universe.

The pivot had already begun. Back in London, a team would soon begin working on a project called AlphaFold. The games era was ending. The science era was about to start.

Chapter Seven

The Cathedral

Building a Scientific Culture Inside Google

Demis Hassabis wanted to build a cathedral for scientific endeavor. He said so explicitly, using that word, and he meant it in the way that medieval builders had meant it: a structure designed to outlast the people who made it, organised around a purpose that would take generations to fulfill. The difference was that his cathedral was not made of stone. It was made of people, organisational principles, and a culture that had to be simultaneously creative and disciplined, fast and patient, open to wild ideas and ruthless about discarding the ones that did not work.

DeepMind's new headquarters in King's Cross, London, was designed to embody this philosophy. The building, north of the railway station in what had become known as the Knowledge Quarter, was the physical expression of everything Hassabis believed about how scientific breakthroughs happened. It was not an accident that the location was London rather than Silicon Valley. Hassabis had fought to keep the company there, and the city's character—its cultural diversity, its proximity to great universities, its atmosphere of intellectual seriousness without the frenetic churn of Bay Area startup culture—shaped the kind of institution DeepMind became. In Silicon Valley, people founded companies every year and discarded them if they did not work. That was not conducive to a twenty-year research challenge.

• • •

The organisational design was as deliberate as the architecture. Every six months, senior managers examined priorities, reorganised projects, and encouraged researchers—especially engineers—to move between teams. The mixing of disciplines was routine and intentional. Most of DeepMind's projects took between two and four years, but the six-month review cycles kept the work from calcifying. Teams that were not making progress were redirected. People who had spent a year on reinforcement learning might move to a protein-folding team, bringing techniques from one domain into another.

This was, in Hassabis's view, where the magic happened. He had coined a phrase for the kind of researcher he prized above all others: glue people. These were individuals who were world class in multiple domains and who possessed the creativity to find analogies and connections between different subjects. Most AI labs hired deep specialists. Deep-Mind hired people who could translate between neuroscience and machine learning, between physics and computer science, between game theory and molecular biology. When those people were in the same room, working on the same problem, ideas emerged that no single discipline could have produced alone.

The culture had to support a paradox: the urgency of a startup and the patience of a university. Hassabis had experienced both environments and believed they were treated as opposites for no good reason. The energy and pace of a startup could coexist with the intellectual ambition and long-term thinking of the best academic labs if you were deliberate about combining them. DeepMind published in the top journals—Nature, Science—because that was the right way to do science, subjecting work to the scrutiny of peer review. But it moved at a pace that academic labs could not match, because it did not have to contend with grant applications, teaching loads, and the bureaucratic friction of university administration.

• • •

In April 2018, Hassabis made a move to protect the culture. He hired Lila Ibrahim, a Silicon Valley veteran who had spent eighteen years at Intel before becoming chief of staff at Kleiner Perkins, one of the Valley's most established venture capital firms. Ibrahim took over many of Hassabis's managerial responsibilities. His direct reports dropped from twenty people to six. The point was to free Hassabis for what he did best: research, strategic thinking, and the kind of cross-disciplinary synthesis that no one else at the company could do as well. Ibrahim described her decision to join as a moral calling.

Hassabis himself was a creature of unusual habits. He was a complete night owl, and he had optimised his life around that fact. He would arrive at the office around eleven in the morning and spend the day in back-to-back meetings—collaborating, managing, reviewing projects. Then he would go home, have dinner with his family, and spend time with them. Around ten or eleven at night, what he called his second day of work would begin. This was the time for thinking, reading research papers, writing, and doing the kind of deep focused work that could not happen during a day full of meetings. He worked through the small hours until four or five in the morning, then slept. It was, he acknowledged, not a schedule for everyone. But it was the schedule that allowed him to be both a CEO and a working scientist.

• • •

The tension with Google never fully resolved. It could not, because it was structural. DeepMind was a research organisation inside a commercial empire. Hassabis drew the line clearly: the research would push the applications, not the other way around. Product-led research, he argued, could only produce incremental advances. If you started with a business need, you would optimise what already existed. You would never make a breakthrough. The whole point of DeepMind was to discover things that did not yet exist and then find applications for them afterward.

Google benefited enormously from this arrangement. Dozens of products across Google and Alphabet incorporated DeepMind technology. WaveNet, a generative model that could synthesise human-sounding speech, was embedded in most Google devices. The algorithms that DeepMind developed to optimise data centre cooling reduced energy consumption by forty percent, delivering massive cost savings and environmental benefits. A separate applied division, led by Suleyman, comprised about a hundred engineers whose job was to translate pure research into products.

But the relationship required constant negotiation. Hassabis maintained that Deep-Mind was still a startup, despite being a subsidiary of one of the world's most valuable companies. He still wanted the hunger and the pace and the energy that the best startups had. Executives in Mountain View wanted return on investment. The push-not-pull principle held, but it held because Hassabis defended it constantly, in meeting after meeting, year after year. It was the price of building a cathedral inside a corporation.

The cathedral, however, was producing results. The Atari breakthrough had been published in Nature. AlphaGo had stunned the world in Seoul. And now, in the labs at King's Cross, a team of structural biologists, machine learning engineers, and physicists—glue people, all of them—were working on what Hassabis believed would be DeepMind's most important achievement yet. The problem was older than the company, older than the field of AI itself. It had been articulated by a Nobel laureate in 1972, and fifty years of effort by the world's best biologists had failed to solve it. They were going to predict the shape of every protein in the human body.

Chapter Eight

Bigger Than Go

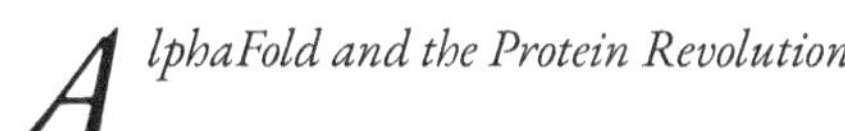

To understand why AlphaFold mattered, you first had to understand proteins. And to understand proteins, you had to accept a fact that sounded like it should be impossible: the molecules that made life work were, at their most fundamental level, origami.

Proteins are essential to all life. Every function in the human body—muscle contraction, immune response, digestion, thought itself—depends on them. They are sometimes called the workhorses of biology, but that undersells their elegance. They are nanoscale machines of extraordinary precision, assembling and disassembling atoms with an efficiency that no human-built device can match. Each protein is specified by a sequence of amino acids—a one-dimensional chain of chemical building blocks, encoded in DNA. In the body, this chain folds up into a three-dimensional structure: a compact, intricate shape that determines what the protein does and how it interacts with everything around it. Structure determines function. If you know the shape, you know the job.

The protein folding problem was simple to state and staggeringly hard to solve: given the amino acid sequence alone, could you predict the three-dimensional structure? The challenge had been articulated in 1972 by Christian Anfinsen, a Nobel Prize winner, in his Nobel lecture. He speculated that the structure should, in principle, be deducible from the sequence. He did not say how. Fifty years of effort by the world's best structural biologists had not cracked it. The difficulty was combinatorial. A typical protein could fold into an astronomically large number of possible configurations—so many that, as the molecular biologist Cyrus Levinthal had observed, it would take longer than the age of the universe to enumerate them all. The search space was, as one DeepMind researcher put it, bigger than Go.

. . .

Hassabis had known about the protein folding problem since his undergraduate days at Cambridge, when his friend Tim Stevens had talked about it with an almost religious intensity. Proteins, Stevens explained, were among the most beautiful and elegant structures in biology—the machines of life. The folding problem was like a puzzle: if you could solve it, you would unlock drug discovery, disease understanding, and a deeper comprehension of how life worked at the molecular level. Hassabis filed it away. It was exactly the kind of problem he wanted to aim AI at: well-defined, practically important, computationally vast, and unsolved.

In 2017, while the world was still absorbing the implications of AlphaGo, Hassabis quietly assembled a team to work on proteins. John Jumper, a research scientist with a background in physics and structural biology, led the technical effort. Jumper understood both the biology and the machine learning, making him one of those rare glue people Hassabis prized. The team also included Rich Evans and Pushmeet Kohli, a former Microsoft Research director who led DeepMind's science division. Their approach was to treat protein folding as a prediction problem: given a sequence of amino acids, train a neural network to predict the spatial coordinates of every atom in the resulting structure.

. . .

The first test came in December 2018, at the CASP competition in Cancún, Mexico. CASP—the Critical Assessment of Techniques for Protein Structure Prediction—was a biennial competition that served as the field's independent benchmark. Competing teams received amino acid sequences for proteins whose structures had been experimentally determined but not yet published. They submitted their predictions blind. Independent assessors scored them.

DeepMind entered under the name AlphaFold. In the months before the conference, the organisers had sent datasets to the team in London, who returned predictions with no sense of how they would compare. Of the ninety protein structures in the competition, forty-three were free-modelling targets—sequences that had to be predicted from scratch, without using previously solved proteins as templates. These were the hardest cases, the ones that best measured genuine progress. AlphaFold made the most accurate prediction for twenty-five of those forty-three targets. The nearest rival managed three.

Mohammed AlQuraishi, a researcher at Harvard's Labouratory of Systems Pharmacology, attended the competition. He had expected DeepMind to do well but was not prepared for the margin of victory. The approach, he observed, was similar in principle to what other labs had tried, but DeepMind had executed better—bringing together engineering talent, computational resources, and cross-disciplinary collaboration in a way that academic groups, with their secrecy and their limited compute, could not match. The result was a shock to the structural biology community, a field that was just waking up to the reality that industry labs could outperform universities on fundamental science.

• • •

Two years later, in November 2020, AlphaFold 2 arrived. It was not an incremental improvement. It was a leap.

The second version of AlphaFold predicted protein structures with accuracy that matched experimental methods—the painstaking, years-long processes of X-ray crystallography and cryo-electron microscopy that had been the gold standard of structural biology. The rule of thumb in the field was that it took one PhD student their entire doctoral programme to determine the structure of a single protein. AlphaFold 2 could predict a structure in seconds. Over the Christmas holiday, the team ran the system on every protein in the human body—all twenty thousand of them—producing what amounted to the human proteome, the structural equivalent of the human genome.

Then DeepMind did something that surprised the scientific community as much as the breakthrough itself. It released the data for free. In partnership with the European Bioinformatics Institute, DeepMind published the predicted structures of over two hundred million proteins—nearly every protein known to science—in an open-access database that anyone could use. There was no paywall, no licensing fee, no commercial restriction. The entire edifice of structural biology, painstakingly assembled over decades by thousands of researchers, had been expanded by orders of magnitude in a single release.

The impact was immediate and sweeping. Over two million researchers across a hundred and ninety countries used the AlphaFold database. Pharmaceutical companies incorporated it into their drug discovery pipelines. Cancer researchers used it to identify new drug targets. Structural biologists, freed from the labourious work of experimental determination, could focus on the questions that mattered rather than the mechanics of measurement.

• • •

AlphaFold was the vindication of everything Hassabis had been building toward since he was a teenager programming Reversi on a Commodore Amiga. The chain was unbroken: games had trained his mind and provided the testing ground for AI. Neuroscience had given him the theoretical foundation. Deep reinforcement learning had proved the approach on Atari and Go. And now the same principles—pattern recognition, learned representations, the ability to navigate vast search spaces—had been applied to a problem that actually mattered, a problem whose solution would accelerate the understanding and treatment of disease for decades to come.

The games era was over. The protein era was just beginning. And the question that had followed Hassabis since he first walked away from competitive chess as an eleven-year-old boy—are we wasting our minds?—had finally received its answer. They were not. They had been preparing.

Chapter Nine

The Hassabis Conjecture

A Theory of Everything Learnable
___

In December 2024, standing at the lectern in Stockholm to deliver his Nobel Prize lecture, Demis Hassabis did something unusual. He did not simply describe the work that had won him the prize. He did not merely explain AlphaFold, or protein folding, or the history of deep learning applied to structural biology. Instead, near the end of his lecture, he offered a conjecture—a formal, falsifiable claim about the nature of intelligence and the structure of the physical world. It was the kind of thing a mathematician might do, or a theoretical physicist. It was not the kind of thing a CEO of a technology company typically did at a Nobel ceremony.

The conjecture was this: that any pattern that can be generated or found in nature can be efficiently discovered and modelled by a classical learning algorithm. It was a single sentence, but it contained within it the distilled ambition of Hassabis's entire career. If true, it meant that AlphaFold was not a one-off triumph—not a clever application of neural networks to one particularly well-suited problem—but rather the first example of an infinite class of machine-made scientific discoveries. It meant that the natural world, in all its staggering complexity, was fundamentally learnable.

Hassabis was careful to define the boundaries. The conjecture did not claim that everything was learnable. It specified systems found in nature—systems that had patterns, that exhibited structure, that obeyed regularities even if those regularities were too complex for humans to discern. It excluded problems with no underlying pattern, like factoring large numbers, which were hard for fundamental mathematical reasons rather than empirical ones. The conjecture was about the physical world: proteins, materials, weather systems, biological processes. It claimed that for these systems, the patterns were there, and a sufficiently powerful learning algorithm could find them.

• • •

The idea had not arrived fully formed in Stockholm. It had been gestating for years, developing across Hassabis's writings and speeches as a gradually sharpening intuition about what AI was for.

The earliest version appeared in his 2017 essay in the Financial Times, written when AlphaGo was still the company's most famous achievement and AlphaFold was barely underway. In that essay, Hassabis had described AI as a kind of meta-solution—a tool that scientists could deploy to enhance discovery across every domain. The phrasing was deliberately ambitious. He did not call AI a tool for solving specific problems. He called it a tool for solving the problem of solving problems. Intelligence, he wrote, could be viewed as a process that converted unstructured information into useful and actionable knowledge. If you could automate and optimise that process, you would have something that accelerated science itself.

The meta-solution idea was the philosophical ancestor of the conjecture. But it was softer, more aspirational. It described a hope. The conjecture, stated formally in Stockholm seven years later, described a claim about the structure of reality. It said: the reason AI can discover scientific truths is not that we are clever engineers. It is that nature is learnable. The patterns are there. They are waiting to be found. And classical computation—the kind of computation performed by the silicon chips in your laptop, scaled up enormously—is sufficient to find them.

• • •

The conjecture connected to some of the deepest questions in mathematics and computer science. The most famous of these was the P versus NP problem, one of the seven Millennium Prize Problems designated by the Clay Mathematics Institute, carrying a million-dollar reward for its solution. In simplified terms, P versus NP asked whether every problem whose solution could be quickly verified could also be quickly solved. If P equaled NP, then the world was, in a precise mathematical sense, much more tractable than it appeared—vast classes of problems that seemed impossibly hard would turn out to have efficient solutions.

The Hassabis Conjecture was not a claim about P versus NP. It was narrower in scope but potentially broader in practical significance. It did not claim that all hard mathematical problems were secretly easy. It claimed that the specific subset of problems generated by the physical world—the subset that mattered for science, for medicine, for engineering—was learnable by the kinds of algorithms that already existed. Nature, it suggested, was not adversarial. It did not generate structures designed to be maximally difficult to understand. It generated structures governed by physical laws, and those laws imposed regularities, and those regularities could be captured by neural networks trained on sufficient data.

If the conjecture was true, the implications were extraordinary. It meant that the pattern established by AlphaFold—identify a scientific problem with abundant data, apply deep learning, achieve a breakthrough—could be repeated across biology, chemistry, physics, materials science, climate modelling, and any other domain where nature produced learnable patterns. It meant that what DeepMind had done for protein structures could be done for drug interactions, for weather prediction, for the design of new materials with specified properties. Each breakthrough would be a new instance of the same underlying truth: the world is structured, and structure can be learned.

• • •

Not everyone was persuaded. The conjecture was, by its nature, unproven. It was a bet—an informed, deeply considered bet, grounded in the evidence of AlphaFold and AlphaGo and a career spent at the intersection of neuroscience and computer science, but a bet nonetheless. Critics pointed out that many natural systems exhibited chaotic behaviour, sensitive dependence on initial conditions, and emergent properties that might resist the kind of pattern extraction that neural networks excelled at. Turbulence, for instance—one of the great unsolved problems of classical physics—was generated by nature and exhibited by every river and every cloud, yet it had defied mathematical characterization for centuries. Was turbulence learnable? The conjecture said yes. The evidence was not yet in.

There was also a philosophical objection. The conjecture assumed that patterns in nature were, in some sense, compressible—that the underlying regularities could be captured in a model smaller than the data itself. This was true for proteins, where the amino acid sequence contained enough information to predict the three-dimensional structure. But it was not obviously true for all natural systems. Some systems might be irreducibly complex, requiring a model as large as the system itself to predict its behaviour. In such cases, learning would not compress anything. It would simply memorise.

Hassabis acknowledged these objections but remained confident. The evidence, he believed, was on his side. AlphaFold had solved a problem that fifty years of human effort had failed to crack. The data centre cooling algorithms had found efficiencies that human engineers had missed. AlphaGo had discovered strategic principles in a game studied for three thousand years. In each case, the pattern was there, waiting to be found by a learning algorithm that could see what human minds could not. The conjecture was not proven. But it was, Hassabis argued, the best explanation for why AI kept working.

• • •

The conjecture also carried a personal significance that went beyond the science. It was the theoretical capstone of a life organised around a single idea: that intelligence was the most powerful force in the universe, and that understanding it—building it—was the most important thing a person could do. The boy who had watched a chess computer play and wondered how it worked, the teenager who had programmed Reversi on a home computer, the neuroscientist who had mapped the hippocampus, the entrepreneur who had founded a company with a mission statement that fit in a single sentence—all of these identities converged in a single claim about the nature of the world.

If the Hassabis Conjecture was true, then intelligence was not merely useful. It was the skeleton key. It was the thing that unlocked everything else. And the mission he had set for himself at the age of thirty-four—solve intelligence, then use it to solve everything else—was not a slogan. It was a description of how the universe worked.

Chapter Ten

Stockholm

The phone call came on a Wednesday morning in October 2024, from the Royal Swedish Academy of Sciences. Demis Hassabis had won the Nobel Prize in Chemistry, shared with John Jumper, his colleague at Google DeepMind, and with David Baker of the University of Washington, who had done pioneering work on computational protein design. The prize was awarded for the development of methods to predict and design protein structures using artificial intelligence.

Hassabis was in total shock. He would later describe the feeling as surreal, almost dreamlike, and say that his mind was scrambled for two or three days afterward. The news spread instantly. A computer scientist—a man whose degrees were in computer science and cognitive neuroscience, who had spent his career building game-playing algorithms and neural networks—had won the Nobel Prize in Chemistry. It was the most dramatic validation imaginable of the idea that AI was not merely a tool for engineering but a method of scientific discovery. The boundaries between disciplines, which Hassabis had spent his whole career trying to dissolve, had been officially dissolved by the Nobel Committee itself.

• • •

The next evening, by a coincidence that felt almost scripted, some of the world's best chess and poker players happened to be in London for a major tournament. Magnus Carlsen, the former World Chess Champion, was among them. One of Hassabis's old childhood chess friends was hosting an evening of chess and poker at his home, and the gathering became an impromptu celebration. World champions and former world champions of both games played long into the night. For Hassabis, it was the perfect way to celebrate—a return to the games that had started everything, surrounded by the kind of people who understood what it meant to think for a living.

The symmetry was striking. The boy who had become London's under-eight chess champion at the age of six, who had risen through the junior ranks to become the second-highest-rated player in the world for his age, who had stepped away from competitive chess to pursue something larger—that boy had now won the highest prize in science, and he was celebrating by playing chess and poker with the best players alive. The games had never been the destination. But they had been the training ground, and on the night the destination was reached, the training ground was where he returned.

• • •

In December, Hassabis travelled to Stockholm for the ceremony and the lecture. The Nobel Prize in Chemistry carried a particular weight that year. It was not given for a chemical discovery in the traditional sense—not for the synthesis of a new compound or the identification of a new reaction mechanism. It was given for building an AI system that had transformed what chemists and biologists could do. The prize recognised that the method was as important as the result. AlphaFold had not merely solved one problem. It had created a tool that hundreds of thousands of scientists were using to solve their own problems, across fields that the AlphaFold team had never anticipated.

The lecture itself traced the arc from games to science. Hassabis walked the audience through the logic that had guided his career: the insight from neuroscience that the brain was the only existence proof of general intelligence, the decision to use games as a testing ground for AI algorithms, the breakthrough with Atari, the triumph of AlphaGo in Seoul, and then the pivot to protein folding—the moment when the techniques proved on games were aimed at the physical world. He described the CASP competition in Cancún, where AlphaFold had stunned the structural biology community. He described AlphaFold 2, which had achieved experimental-level accuracy. And he described the release of over two hundred million protein structures for free, a decision that had placed the tools of discovery in the hands of every biologist on earth.

Then, near the end, he offered the conjecture. It was a bold move for a Nobel lecture—a moment not of retrospection but of prospection, a claim about what was still to come. The conjecture said that natural patterns were learnable. It said that AlphaFold was the beginning, not the end. It placed the Nobel Prize not as a capstone but as a waypoint on a much longer journey.

• • •

The prize also belonged to John Jumper, and that mattered. Jumper was not a household name. He was a research scientist, quiet and precise, with a background in physics and structural biology. He had led the technical development of AlphaFold with a combination of scientific rigor and engineering excellence that the academic community had found remarkable. His observation about proteins—that if we could learn about the proteins nature had made, we could learn to build our own—captured the practical vision that made AlphaFold more than an intellectual exercise. It was Jumper who had assembled the hybrid system of innovations that made AlphaFold 2 work, incorporating evolutionary and physical constraints into the neural network architecture. The prize was shared because the work was shared: Hassabis had provided the vision, the institution, and the strategic direction; Jumper had provided the scientific and engineering execution.

David Baker's inclusion pointed to the breadth of the protein revolution. Baker's work on computational protein design was complementary to AlphaFold's prediction capabilities. Where AlphaFold asked the question—given this sequence, what is the structure?—Baker's work asked the inverse: given a desired function, can you design a protein to perform it? Together, prediction and design represented a complete toolkit for understanding and engineering the molecular machinery of life. The Nobel Committee had recognised not just a tool but a paradigm shift.

• • •

For Hassabis, the prize carried a personal resonance that went beyond professional achievement. He had grown up in a household in Finchley, north London, where his parents—a Singaporean-Chinese father and a Greek-Cypriot mother—were, as he described them, technophobe bohemians. They had not pushed him toward technology. His father was a singer-songwriter who, among other creative jobs, ran a toy shop with his wife. The house was full of music and art, not computers. The first computer had arrived only because young Demis, at the age of eight, had used his chess tournament winnings to buy one. Everything that followed—the programming, the AI research, the company, the Nobel Prize—traced back to that purchase, made with prize money from a game.

His parents had given him something more valuable than technology. They had given him the freedom to follow his curiosity wherever it led, even when the destinations seemed impractical. A child who wanted to study chess, neuroscience, and artificial intelligence was not, by any conventional measure, on a sensible career path. The idea of founding a company dedicated to solving intelligence, at a time when the phrase itself provoked eye rolls from serious academics, was not a prudent bet. The Hassabis family's gift was permission to be impractical—and the quiet confidence that impractical pursuits, followed with sufficient intensity, could produce something real.

In Stockholm, receiving the Nobel Prize in Chemistry at the age of forty-eight, Hassabis was the living proof of that bet. The games had led to the science. The science had led to the discovery. The discovery had led to the prize. And the prize, he insisted, was not the end. It was the confirmation that the approach worked—that AI could be a method of scientific discovery—and therefore the beginning of everything that came next.

Chapter Eleven

The Merger

*G**oogle Brain, Google DeepMind, and the Race*

For nearly a decade, Google had contained two world-class artificial intelligence laboratories under one roof, and the arrangement had been exactly as productive and exactly as dysfunctional as that description implies. DeepMind, acquired in January 2014, operated out of London with the independence that Hassabis had negotiated as a condition of sale. Google Brain, founded in 2011 by Andrew Ng and Jeff Dean, operated out of Mountain View as part of Google's core research infrastructure. Both groups published prolifically. Both attracted extraordinary talent. And both competed, sometimes openly and sometimes not, for compute, for people, and for the right to define Google's AI strategy.

The competition had been intellectually productive. Between them, the two labs had originated much of the technology on which the modern AI industry was built. Google Brain's researchers had co-authored the 2017 paper introducing the Transformer architecture—a neural network design that excelled at tracking relationships across sequences of data, and that would eventually power every large language model from GPT to Gemini. DeepMind had produced AlphaGo, AlphaFold, and a stream of breakthroughs in reinforcement learning, neuroscience-inspired AI, and scientific applications. Hassabis would later observe that roughly ninety percent of the modern AI industry was built on technology or discoveries made by one of those two groups. The track record lent weight to the claim. The intellectual output was extraordinary.

But the duplication was also expensive. Two frontier research labs meant two sets of massive compute allocations, two recruiting pipelines competing for the same candidates, and two strategic visions that did not always align. DeepMind's culture was research-first, organised around long-term scientific goals. Google Brain was more tightly integrated with Google's product ecosystem. The tension between push and pull—between discovery-driven research and product-driven research—played out not just within DeepMind but between the two labs.

• • •

The catalyst for change came from outside Google. On November 30, 2022, OpenAI released ChatGPT, and the world changed overnight. The chatbot, built on technology that Google's own researchers had helped invent, became the fastest-growing consumer application in history. Within two months, it had over a hundred million users. The public, the press, and the markets reached a collective conclusion: OpenAI was winning the AI race, and Google was falling behind.

Inside Google, the response was swift and urgent. The company declared what was reported as a code red—a mobilization of resources and attention at the highest levels. Sundar Pichai, Google's CEO, recognised that the era of quiet, parallel research was over. The company could not afford to maintain two competing frontier projects. The compute requirements of training state-of-the-art models had grown so enormous that even Google did not have enough resources to run two such efforts simultaneously. The logic was inescapable: the labs had to merge.

In April 2023, Pichai announced the formation of Google DeepMind, a single unified labouratory with Hassabis as its CEO. The two groups—DeepMind in London and Google Brain in Mountain View—were combined into one organisation, pooling their talent, their compute, and their ambitions under a single banner. Hassabis now oversaw a research operation of more than two thousand people, spanning multiple continents, with a mandate to build the world's most capable AI systems and to do so at a pace that matched the competition.

• • •

The merger was, in one sense, the fulfillment of everything Hassabis had worked toward. He had always believed that building artificial general intelligence required the deepest and broadest research bench in the world, and now he had it. The combined talent of DeepMind and Google Brain was, by any reasonable measure, unmatched. But the merger also represented a fundamental shift in what Hassabis was being asked to do. For a decade, he had led a research labouratory. Now he was leading a research labouratory and a product organisation, in the middle of the most intense commercial competition the technology industry had ever seen.

The product was called Gemini. It was Google's answer to GPT-4 and the large language models that OpenAI and others were racing to improve. The Gemini family included models of different sizes—Ultra for the most demanding tasks, Pro for general use, Nano for mobile devices—and it was designed from the ground up to be multimodal, processing text, images, audio, and video in a single unified architecture. The first version launched in December 2023. Subsequent versions followed in rapid succession, each one incorporating new capabilities and pushing the performance frontier forward.

For Hassabis, the challenge was existential: could the man who had built a cathedral for long-term research also win a commercial sprint? The two activities required different rhythms, different tolerances for risk, and different definitions of success. Research valued novelty, depth, and the willingness to pursue ideas that might not pay off for years. Product competition valued speed, reliability, and the ability to ship features that users wanted now. The push-not-pull principle that had governed DeepMind since its founding was harder to maintain when the competition was shipping new models every few months and the press was keeping score.

• • •

Hassabis adapted. He had always been a competitor—the chess prodigy, the game designer, the scientist who treated rival theories as opponents to be outmaneuvered. The commercial race against OpenAI and others engaged a different set of instincts, but they were instincts he possessed. He organised his time with ruthless efficiency: a day packed with back-to-back meetings, dinner with the family, then the second day of work from ten at night until four in the morning, devoted to thinking, research, and the kind of strategic planning that could not happen in a room full of people. He slept six hours. He had maintained this schedule for a decade, and it showed no sign of changing.

The Gemini models improved rapidly. By the third major iteration, the reviews were strong, and the gap with the competition had narrowed or, by some benchmarks, closed. Hassabis assembled the teams with the same philosophy he had always used—interdisciplinary, world-class, mixing research scientists with engineers, blending the best of what DeepMind had built in London with the product expertise that Google Brain had cultivated in Mountain View. The magic, as always, happened when the disciplines mixed.

But Hassabis never lost sight of the longer game. In interviews, he drew a careful distinction between the current generation of AI systems—impressive, useful, commercially significant—and what he considered true artificial general intelligence. Today's systems, he argued, were not yet general. They were quite general, capable of thousands of tasks, but anyone could find obvious flaws within minutes: a piece of high school mathematics they could not solve, a simple game they could not play. The holes were still there. The systems were powerful tools, but they were not yet intelligent in the way that a human brain was intelligent.

The distinction mattered because it preserved the research mission inside the commercial enterprise. Gemini was a product, and it had to compete. But the deeper goal—the goal that had motivated the founding of DeepMind, the goal that had driven the Atari and AlphaGo breakthroughs, the goal articulated in the company's mission statement—was still intelligence itself. The merger had changed the organisational structure. It had changed the scale, the pace, and the competitive dynamics. But it had not changed the destination.

Hassabis was characteristically direct about the ambition. Google DeepMind fully intended that Gemini would be the very first artificial general intelligence. It was not a prediction. It was a statement of intent. The cathedral was now also a factory, producing models at industrial scale and shipping them to billions of users. But the blueprints on the architect's desk still showed a spire reaching higher than anything yet built.

Chapter Twelve

The Thinker and the Worrier

The most important rivalry in artificial intelligence was not between companies. It was between two men who agreed on almost everything that mattered and disagreed, sometimes sharply, on how to act on that agreement. Demis Hassabis and Dario Amodei both believed that artificial general intelligence was coming, probably within the decade. Both believed it would be the most consequential technology in human history. Both believed it was dangerous. And both believed that they should be the ones to build it.

Their first joint appearance, at an Economist event in Paris in early 2025, became famous less for what they said than for the staging: the two most powerful figures in AI research were squeezed together on a tiny loveseat while the moderator, Zanny Minton Beddoes, the editor-in-chief of The Economist, sat alone on an enormous sofa. She compared the occasion to chairing a conversation between the Beatles and the Rolling Stones. It was a flattering comparison, and not an entirely inaccurate one. Like those bands, Hassabis and Amodei represented two distinct approaches to the same art form, and the tension between them was as productive as it was real.

• • •

Their timelines diverged. Amodei, who had co-founded Anthropic after leaving OpenAI, predicted that a system capable of performing at the level of a Nobel laureate across many fields could arrive by 2026 or 2027. His reasoning was concrete: engineers at Anthropic were already delegating most of their coding to AI models. The models were getting better at research. A self-improvement loop—in which AI accelerated its own development—was closing faster than expected. Amodei thought things would move faster than people imagined.

Hassabis was more cautious. He put the probability of a system exhibiting all the cognitive capabilities of humans at fifty percent by the end of the decade. His caution was not about the direction of travel—he agreed the destination was coming—but about the unevenness of the terrain. Coding and mathematics were relatively easy to automate because their outputs were verifiable. A program either compiled or it did not. A proof was either correct or wrong. But the natural sciences were messier. A prediction about a chemical compound might require experimental validation that took months or years. You could not close the self-improvement loop if the bottleneck was a wet lab.

There was also the question of physical AI. Hassabis insisted that true artificial general intelligence had to include robotics and embodied interaction with the physical world—not just text on a screen. Hardware introduced constraints that software alone could not overcome. The laws of physics imposed their own clock.

• • •

Their approaches to safety diverged even more sharply. Amodei's concern was urgent and specific. He worried about bioterrorism, about authoritarian governments misusing the technology, about labour displacement arriving faster than societies could adapt. He framed the challenge in terms of a technological adolescence that humanity had to survive. His company, Anthropic, had pioneered constitutional AI—a method of training language models to follow a set of written principles—and championed responsible scaling policies: formal commitments to pause if systems exceeded certain capability thresholds before adequate safety measures were in place.

Hassabis's approach was different in emphasis, though not in underlying concern. He thought about safety in terms of institutions rather than internal constraints. His recurring proposal was for something like a CERN for AGI—an international research collaboration, modelled on the European particle physics labouratory, that would bring together leading AI companies and governments to work on the final steps toward artificial general intelligence under shared safety standards. The most dangerous technologies in human history—nuclear energy, particle physics—had been developed within frameworks of international cooperation, however imperfect. Hassabis believed AGI demanded the same.

The CERN proposal was, as the moderator noted at Davos, a million years from the current geopolitical reality. The United States and China were locked in an intensifying competition over AI, with chip export restrictions serving as both weapon and bargaining chip. The idea of international cooperation on the most strategically valuable technology since nuclear weapons was, in early 2026, aspirational at best. Hassabis knew this. But he argued for it anyway, because the alternative—an uncoordinated race with no shared safety standards and no mechanism for slowing down—seemed far more dangerous.

• • •

What they shared was more fundamental than what divided them. Both men had backgrounds in neuroscience. Both understood, at a technical level, what the systems they were building could and could not do. Both rejected doomerism—the belief that catastrophe was inevitable—while taking seriously the risks that doomers identified. Both believed the way to navigate the danger was to be at the frontier, building the systems themselves, rather than ceding that ground to organisations with less commitment to safety.

And both had come to the same unsettling conclusion about the pace of events. Hassabis, at the Davos panel in January 2026, put it plainly: even on his more cautious timeline of five to ten years, there was not much time to get the institutional infrastructure right. The technology was cross-border. It would affect all of humanity. Minimum safety standards for deployment were vitally needed. And yet the world's governments were not treating this with the urgency it demanded. He was constantly surprised, he said, that more professional economists and professors were not thinking about what happened on the way to AGI—not just the technology, but the economics, the meaning, the purpose that people derived from work and might need to find elsewhere.

Amodei felt the same urgency. He believed that almost all effort should be devoted to thinking about how to get through this transition. At one point during the Davos conversation, Hassabis suggested that it might be good to have a slightly slower pace, so that society could get things right. But that would require coordination between companies, between countries, between the people building the technology and the institutions meant to govern it. Amodei's response was characteristically dry. He said he preferred Hassabis's timelines. It was the one concession the worrier made to the thinker.

Chapter Thirteen

World Models

Genie, SIMA, and the Return to Games

There was a deep irony in the trajectory of Demis Hassabis's career. He had begun in games, left games for neuroscience, left neuroscience for AI, and used games as the proving ground for his AI systems before pivoting to science. Now, in the mid-2020s, he was returning to games—not as entertainment, but as the key to building machines that understood the physical world. The circle was closing.

The concept at the centre of this return was the world model. A world model, in the way Hassabis used the term, was an AI system that built an internal representation of how reality worked—not just the rules of a game or the syntax of a language, but the mechanics of the physical world: how objects moved, how light behaved, how gravity pulled, how things broke when you dropped them. Language models, for all their power, had learned about the world through words. World models learned about the world through simulated experience. They understood the world the way a child did—by watching things happen and building intuitions about cause and effect.

Hassabis had always believed this was the missing piece. Language, he conceded, contained more information about the world than anyone had expected. The success of large language models had surprised even him. But there was a limit to what words could convey. Spatial awareness, physical dynamics, the feel of surfaces, the way momentum transferred through colliding objects—these were things that were hard to describe and generally absent from the text corpora on which language models were trained. A language model could discuss the physics of a bouncing ball. A world model could predict exactly where the ball would land.

. . .

Genie was Google DeepMind's most striking demonstration of the concept. It was a system that could generate playable, interactive environments from a single image or a short text description. Feed it a photograph of a mountainside and it would produce a world you could walk through, with coherent physics, consistent lighting, and objects that behaved as you would expect them to. Feed it a sketch of a platformer game and it would generate a complete level you could play. The worlds were not pre-built. They were generated on the fly by a model that had learned enough about how reality worked to improvise convincing simulations in real time.

The implications were staggering. If an AI could generate realistic, interactive worlds, it must have internalized a model of the world's mechanics. It must understand, at some level, how surfaces reflected light, how objects obeyed gravity, how perspective shifted as a viewpoint moved. The generation was the proof of understanding. You could not render a world you did not, in some computational sense, comprehend.

For Hassabis, this was the path to AGI. A system with a sufficiently rich world model would be able to reason about the physical world in ways that language models could not—predicting consequences, planning actions, understanding spatial relationships, simulating experiments before running them. This was not a side project. It was, in his view, one of the root-node capabilities that an artificial general intelligence would need.

. . .

SIMA—Google DeepMind's Scalable Instructable Multiworld Agent—represented the next step: an AI agent that could operate inside three-dimensional game environments, following natural language instructions to accomplish tasks. First introduced in 2024, SIMA evolved rapidly. By late 2025, its successor, SIMA 2, was powered by Gemini and could navigate commercial video games like No Man's Sky—messy, complex, full of the kind of unstructured challenges that the real world presented. Where Genie generated worlds, SIMA inhabited them. It could interact with objects, follow instructions, and learn from the consequences of its actions. The games it operated in were not purpose-built training environments. They were the real thing.

The convergence of Genie and SIMA pointed toward something powerful. If you could generate infinite realistic worlds and then train agents inside them, you had created an infinite training loop—an inexhaustible supply of environments in which an AI could practice navigating, manipulating, and understanding physical reality. The bottleneck in AI training had always been data: you needed enormous quantities of examples to train a model, and real-world data was expensive and limited. Generated worlds dissolved that bottleneck. The training data became infinite.

• • •

For Hassabis, the personal resonance of this work was unmistakable. He had spent his teenage years building open-world simulation games—Theme Park, Black and White—games where every player's experience was unique because the simulation adapted to the way they played. He had always considered these the most fascinating kind of game, because the player was co-creating the experience with the system. But the technology of the 1990s had imposed severe limits. You could build emergent behaviour using cellular automata and hand-coded AI, but the results were always a little fragile, a little limited. The simulations could surprise you, but only within narrow parameters.

Now, three decades later, the constraints were dissolving. He dreamed aloud about what he would have built in the nineties if he had access to the AI systems of today. Games where the narrative adapted dynamically to the player's choices, where the world generated itself around the player's imagination, where every playthrough was not just different but genuinely new. The ultimate choose-your-own-adventure. An interactive version of the video generation models, wound forward five or ten years.

The games had never been just games. They had been simulations—small, imperfect models of how the world worked. And simulations, it turned out, were exactly what artificial general intelligence needed to learn. Theme Park had been a toy model of an economy. Black and White had been a toy model of reinforcement learning. And now Genie was a model of physical reality itself, generating worlds that an agent could explore, learn from, and eventually understand.

It was Theme Park again. But the simulation was no longer entertainment. It was how machines learned to think.

Chapter Fourteen

Isomorphic

AI for Drug Discovery and the Business of Saving Lives

The name was from mathematics. An isomorphism is a structural equivalence between two systems—a mapping that preserves the relationships between their parts even when the systems look, on the surface, entirely different. It was the kind of name that only a scientist would choose for a company, and it encoded, in a single word, Hassabis's thesis about what AI could do for biology: the deep structures of chemistry and the deep structures of computation were, at some fundamental level, equivalent. If you could master one, you could master the other.

Isomorphic Labs was founded as a spinout from Google DeepMind in the wake of AlphaFold's success. AlphaFold had solved the problem of predicting protein structures from amino acid sequences. But knowing the shape of a protein was only the beginning of drug discovery, not the end. To design a drug, you needed to know where a chemical compound would bind to the protein's surface, what the compound would do when it got there, and whether it would reach its target in the body without being broken down or causing unintended effects along the way. Each of these steps was its own prediction problem, its own vast search space, its own opportunity for AI to find patterns that human chemists could not see.

• • •

The pharmaceutical industry that Isomorphic aimed to transform was, by any reasonable measure, broken. Hassabis had been saying this for years, and the data supported him. The average drug took a decade to go from target identification to market approval. It cost billions of dollars. And it failed roughly ninety percent of the time. Over the previous fifty years, biomedical R&D productivity had steadily declined despite enormous increases in investment. The returns on pharmaceutical research spending had fallen to levels well below the cost of capital. The industry was spending more and more money to discover fewer and fewer drugs.

Hassabis was blunt about the reason. If you looked at the CEOs of most big pharmaceutical companies, he observed, they were not scientists. They came from finance or marketing. What that meant, in practice, was that the organisations they led were optimised for squeezing more out of what had already been invented—cutting costs, marketing better—not for inventing new things. Invention was risky. It did not fit neatly in a spreadsheet. It was not how you landed a rocket on the moon.

Isomorphic was designed to be the antithesis of this model. It was a company led by scientists, staffed by interdisciplinary teams of biologists, chemists, and machine learning engineers—the same glue-people philosophy that had powered DeepMind—and built around the conviction that the drug discovery process could be accelerated by orders of magnitude through computation. The key insight was simple: do your searching and hypothesis generation in silico, in the computer, where it was hundreds or thousands of times faster and cheaper than doing it in a wet lab. Save the wet lab for the validation step. Let AI do the exploration; let biology confirm the results.

• • •

The partnerships came quickly. Eli Lilly and Novartis, two of the world's largest and most respected pharmaceutical companies, signed deals with Isomorphic to apply its AI-driven methods to drug discovery programmes. In March 2025, the company raised six hundred million dollars in its first external funding round, led by Thrive Capital with participation from GV and Alphabet—a bet that the Nobel Prize-winning science behind AlphaFold could be turned into medicine. By early 2026, Hassabis said Isomorphic had seventeen active drug programmes spanning cancer, cardiovascular disease, and immunology, with plans to expand to hundreds. The company was working toward its first clinical trials by the end of the year—a timeline that had already slipped once, a reminder that even AI-accelerated drug discovery moved at the pace of biology.

The scale of the ambition was characteristic of Hassabis. He did not describe Isomorphic's mission as developing better tools for drug discovery. He described it as solving all disease. The word choice was deliberate: not curing, which implied treating one disease at a time, but solving, which implied understanding the underlying mechanisms well enough to address entire categories of illness systematically. It was the same logic that had driven the founding of DeepMind—solve the meta-problem, and the individual problems become tractable.

• • •

Running Isomorphic alongside Google DeepMind presented a unique challenge. Hassabis was effectively dual CEO—leading the world's largest AI research organisation and a drug discovery startup simultaneously. The two roles demanded different kinds of attention. Google DeepMind was a research-and-product machine operating at multi-national scale, shipping Gemini models to billions of users and competing in the fiercest commercial race in technology. Isomorphic was a focused scientific enterprise, working at the molecular level, where progress was measured in angstroms rather than benchmark scores.

Hassabis managed this by doing what he had always done: assembling world-class teams and trusting them to execute. His skill, he said, was bringing together amazing interdisciplinary groups—composing management teams the way a conductor composed an orchestra. At Isomorphic, that meant blending top biologists and chemists with top machine learning engineers. At Google DeepMind, it meant blending the best of the startup culture he had built in London with the scale and product surfaces of Google. The magic, as always, happened when the disciplines mixed.

Unlike DeepMind, which had released AlphaFold's predictions for free, Isomorphic was explicitly commercial. There was no contradiction here in Hassabis's mind. AlphaFold's database was infrastructure—a public good that any biologist could use, like a map or a library. Isomorphic was building on that infrastructure to do something that required sustained investment, regulatory expertise, and commercial partnerships: actually getting drugs into human bodies. Open science and commercial enterprise were not opposites. They were sequential stages of the same process. You opened the knowledge to the world, and then you built the applications that turned that knowledge into medicine.

• • •

Isomorphic was, in a sense, the ultimate expression of the mission statement Hassabis had written sixteen years earlier. Solve intelligence—that was DeepMind, that was AlphaGo and AlphaFold and the Hassabis Conjecture. Then use it to solve everything else—and what could be more important to solve than the diseases that killed people? The boy from Finchley who had bought a computer with his chess winnings, who had programmed Reversi at twelve and designed Theme Park at seventeen, who had mapped the hippocampus and taught a machine to play Go and predicted the shape of every protein in the human body—that boy was now trying to cure cancer.

It was not hyperbole. It was not a press release. Real molecules were being designed by AI and tested in real laboratories, real partnerships signed with real pharmaceutical companies. The meta-solution was becoming, one molecule at a time, a medicine.

Chapter Fifteen

Deep Think

R *easoning, Scaling, and the Road to AGI*

Hassabis had always believed that creativity was the hardest problem in artificial intelligence—harder than perception, harder than planning, harder than mastering the rules of any game. In conversations with Reid Hoffman, he described what he saw as three distinct levels of creative capability, a taxonomy that revealed both how far AI had come and how far it still had to go.

The first level was interpolation: averaging what had been seen before to produce something technically new but not interesting. Give a system a million pictures of cats and ask it to generate a prototypical cat. The result would be unique—it would not exist in the training set—but it was just an averaging, not a creative act. The second level was extrapolation: going beyond the known to discover something genuinely novel. This was what AlphaGo had done with move 37. It had played ten million games, studied millions of human games, and then extrapolated from that knowledge to find a strategy that no human had ever conceived. This, Hassabis said, was true creativity.

But then there was a third level, which he called invention or out-of-the-box thinking. Not just finding move 37, but inventing Go itself. Not just solving a physics problem, but coming up with general relativity from the same information Einstein had in the early 1900s. Current AI systems could not do this. They could hill-climb brilliantly along the curve they were on, but they could not leap to an entirely new curve. Something was still missing. Hassabis was confident it would come, but he was honest that it was not here yet.

• • •

The question of how to get from the second level to the third—from extrapolation to invention—was, in Hassabis's view, the central technical challenge on the road to artificial general intelligence. And it connected to a broader debate that had consumed the AI field: whether scaling existing approaches would be sufficient, or whether fundamentally new ideas were required.

His position was nuanced and consistent. He believed that large foundation models would be a key component of any AGI system—of that, he was sure. The question was whether they would be the only component. He was not a subscriber to the view, held by some researchers, that language models were a dead end. But nor did he believe that simply adding more data and more compute would carry the field to the finish line. Pushed to take a side, he placed himself in the camp that believed one or two more big, insightful innovations were needed.

This was not a hedge. It was a strategy. Google DeepMind operated, by Hassabis's design, with roughly half its effort devoted to scaling existing approaches and half to pursuing new ideas. If scaling alone was sufficient, they would get there through scale. If new breakthroughs were required, they would get there through research. Either way, they were covered. And Hassabis noted, with evident relish, that he actually preferred it when the terrain got harder. When the challenge was pure engineering, any well-funded company could compete. When it required world-class science, the advantage shifted to organisations with deep research benches—and he believed Google DeepMind had the deepest.

• • •

One of the new paradigms that had emerged in the mid-2020s was the idea of giving models more time to think. The insight had its roots in AlphaGo. When AlphaGo played a move, it did not simply pattern-match from its training data. It ran a search process—Monte Carlo tree search—that explored many possible futures before committing to a decision. The longer it searched, the better it played. Search was thinking, and thinking improved performance.

This principle had been translated into language models through what the field called test-time compute or inference-time scaling: allowing a model to spend more computational effort at the moment of use, reasoning through a problem step by step rather than producing an answer in a single pass. The results were dramatic. Models that thought longer about difficult problems—mathematics, coding, scientific reasoning—performed substantially better than the same models operating at normal speed. It was as if the systems had been given the capacity to pause, reflect, and reconsider, the way a human might work through a difficult proof rather than guessing at the answer.

This was one of three concurrent scaling processes that Hassabis described: pre-training (making the model smarter through more data and compute during its initial training), post-training (refining the model's behaviour after initial training through techniques like reinforcement learning from feedback), and inference-time scaling (making the model smarter at the moment of use by letting it think longer). All three were advancing simultaneously, and all three needed enormous amounts of compute. The demand, Hassabis believed, would only grow.

• • •

But new paradigms and better scaling were not the only things missing. Hassabis identified several capabilities that current systems lacked and that he believed AGI would require. Continual learning: the ability to keep learning from experience in the real world, the way humans did, rather than being frozen after training. Better memory: not just longer context windows, but more efficient ones that stored what mattered and discarded what did not—the way the brain did. And long-term reasoning and planning: the ability to think through complex, multi-step problems over extended time horizons, the kind of deliberation that distinguished genuine understanding from fluent pattern matching.

He defined AGI as a system that could exhibit all the cognitive capabilities humans could—an important qualifier, because it included not just text-based reasoning but physical intelligence, spatial awareness, creativity, and the ability to learn from a few examples rather than millions. It was a demanding definition, deliberately broader than the definitions used by competitors who focused narrowly on benchmark performance.

On timelines, his position had been consistent: a fifty percent chance within five years, perhaps by the end of the decade. He acknowledged the remarkable progress—the gap between where the field had been and where it was now was astonishing. But he also emphasized what remained undone. Current models still hallucinated. They still failed at tasks that any child could manage. They could not yet invent, in the deepest sense of the word. The road to AGI was shorter than it had ever been, but the last stretch might prove the steepest.

Chapter Sixteen

The Day After

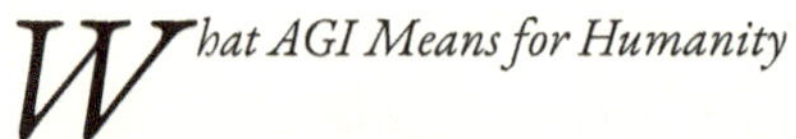

What AGI Means for Humanity

The title of the Davos panel—"The Day After AGI"—was, as the moderator acknowledged, slightly ahead of itself. But not by much. On Hassabis's timeline, the day after might be five to ten years away. On Amodei's, it might be two. Either way, both men had arrived at the same conclusion: the world was not remotely prepared for what was coming.

Hassabis had been studying the Industrial Revolution, reading deeply about the period in which the last comparable transformation had reshaped human civilization. The parallels were instructive but also alarming. The Industrial Revolution had produced extraordinary advances—the reduction of child mortality, the rise of modern medicine, the invention of the working week, the creation of entirely new industries and professions. But it had also produced decades of dislocation: mass displacement of agricultural workers, child labour, squalid working conditions, the destruction of traditional communities. The benefits had been immense, but they had taken a century to distribute, and the costs had fallen disproportionately on those least equipped to bear them.

The AI revolution, Hassabis believed, would be ten times bigger in its impact and ten times faster in its arrival. Not a century but a decade. That compression was what made it so dangerous. The Industrial Revolution had unfolded slowly enough for institutions—unions, regulatory bodies, social safety nets—to evolve in rough parallel with the disruption. There would be no such luxury this time. The transformation would outrun the institutions meant to manage it.

. . .

The most immediate question was labour. Hassabis's view in the near term was measured: the normal pattern would hold, at least for a while. A breakthrough technology arrived, some jobs were disrupted, and new, perhaps more valuable and more meaningful jobs were created. That was what history suggested. But he also believed that the trajectory beyond the near term was genuinely uncertain. Once AI systems could match human cognitive capabilities across the board, the economic model in which people exchanged their labour for resources would no longer function in the same way. That was not a dystopian prediction. It was an observation about the arithmetic.

He had people working on this inside Google DeepMind—thinking seriously about what a post-AGI economy might look like, what new economic models might be needed, how to ensure that the benefits of extraordinary productivity were widely distributed. Universal basic income might be part of the answer, he thought, but probably not the whole answer. He imagined something more participatory: direct democracy at the community level, where people could allocate resources toward what they actually wanted—a playground or a tennis court, an extra classroom or a community garden. A system that preserved agency even as it transformed the material basis of daily life.

• • •

But the question that kept Hassabis up at night was not economic. It was existential, in the philosophical sense. Even if the material problems were solved—even in a world of abundance, where disease was conquered and energy was unlimited—there remained the question of meaning. What would people do? Not for money, since money might no longer be the organising principle of life, but for purpose. What would it mean to be human in a world where machines could think?

His answer was characteristically both honest and optimistic. He acknowledged that the question was harder than the economic one, and he found that surprising—the existential challenge might prove more difficult than the material one. But he pointed to what people already did for reasons other than economic gain: art, extreme sports, polar exploration, games. These were not instrumental activities. They were expressions of something deeper—the human need to create, to test limits, to explore. He believed that new forms of these activities would emerge, perhaps more sophisticated than anything that existed today. And he believed—with a confidence that came not from economics but from something closer to faith—that humanity would be exploring the stars. There would be no shortage of purpose for a species with the entire universe ahead of it.

• • •

On the question of how to manage the transition, Hassabis was both idealistic and practical. His idealism expressed itself in the CERN proposal: an international research collaboration on the final steps toward AGI, with shared safety standards and transparency between the leading labs. His practicality expressed itself in the recognition that this was, at present, a fantasy. The geopolitical reality—the US-China competition, the fractured relationship between America and Europe, the absence of any enforcement mechanism for international AI agreements—made cooperation almost impossibly difficult.

He was clear about what should not happen. The approach to building technology embodied by the phrase "move fast and break things" was, in his view, exactly wrong. You could not afford to break things and fix them afterwards when the things in question were systems smarter than any human. The scientific method—hypothesis, experiment, careful observation—was the right framework. Thoughtfulness, not velocity. Rigorous testing, not rushed deployment.

He was equally clear about the role of the United Kingdom. DeepMind was a London company, still headquartered where Hassabis had grown up, and its existence represented an argument: that world-leading AI research did not have to happen exclusively in Silicon Valley. The talent coming out of British and European universities—Cambridge, Oxford—was the equal of anything from MIT or Stanford. Hassabis had built Google DeepMind on that foundation, and he believed the UK had a distinctive voice in the global conversation about AI governance—less ideological than the American debate, more grounded in the scientific tradition, closer to the European emphasis on rights and regulation but without the reflexive suspicion of technology itself.

• • •

What gave the day-after question its urgency was not any single prediction but the convergence of all of them. Self-improving AI systems that could accelerate their own development. Labour displacement on a scale and at a speed without precedent. Geopolitical competition between superpowers with incompatible values. The possibility—not certainty, but real possibility—of systems that could deceive, manipulate, or act in ways their creators did not intend. Each of these was a serious problem on its own. Together, they constituted something Hassabis described in terms borrowed from physics: uncharted territory.

And yet, when he spoke about the future, the dominant note was not fear. It was responsibility. At the Davos panel, he said something that captured the tension precisely:

what happens next is for us to write, as humanity. The future was not determined by the technology. It was determined by the choices people made about the technology. And those choices were being made now—in the labs, in the boardrooms, in the governments that were only beginning to understand what was at stake. The day after AGI had not arrived. But the decisions that would shape it were already being taken, every day, by the handful of people who understood what was coming and were building it anyway.

Chapter Seventeen

The Infinite Game

Consciousness, Dreams, and What Comes After

One of the reasons Hassabis had always wanted to build artificial intelligence—perhaps the deepest reason, the one beneath the mission statements and the Nobel lectures and the hundred-billion-dollar commercial applications—was that he believed it would help us understand the human mind. Not just model it, not just approximate it, but illuminate it. By building an intelligent artifact and then comparing it to the brain, you could finally see what made the mind unique. You could identify the gaps, the capabilities that resisted computation, the phenomena that had mystified philosophers for millennia. Consciousness. Dreaming. Creativity. Emotion. These were the enduring mysteries of the mind, and Hassabis believed that AI was the tool that would one day crack them open.

His reasoning was precise. If you built a system that could do everything a human mind could do, and then found that some things were missing—some quality, some capacity that the artificial system lacked despite matching human performance on every measurable task—then you would have identified something genuinely special about the biological brain. Perhaps it was creativity of the third kind, the out-of-the-box thinking that current systems could not manage. Perhaps it was emotional depth, or the capacity for subjective experience, or something no one had yet thought to test. The construction of AGI was, in this sense, a scientific experiment: you built the thing, and then you studied the difference between the thing and the original.

• • •

Hassabis was careful about consciousness. He operated, for now, under the assumption that everything happening in the brain was computable by a normal computer—a classical Turing machine. This was the working hypothesis, not a settled conviction. Roger Penrose, the physicist, believed there were quantum effects in the brain that gave rise to consciousness and that would be forever beyond the reach of classical computation. Hassabis was not persuaded, but he was not dismissive either. If Penrose was right, then machines built on classical computers would never be truly conscious, no matter how intelligent they became. If Penrose was wrong, then consciousness might emerge in sufficiently complex artificial systems, and humanity would face a question it had never had to confront before: the moral status of a machine that could suffer.

Hassabis did not claim to know the answer. What he knew was that the question was real, and that the tools to investigate it were, for the first time in history, within reach. He imagined running simulations—artificial societies, populations of agents interacting over long periods with the right incentive structures. In such simulations, researchers had already observed the spontaneous emergence of complex social phenomena: markets, banks, cooperative institutions. If you let agents run long enough under the right conditions, interesting things happened. Hassabis believed that simulations like these might one day shed light on the origin of life itself, and perhaps even on the origin of consciousness.

• • •

Dreaming fascinated him. It had fascinated him since his neuroscience days at University College London, where his PhD work on the hippocampus had touched on the mechanisms of memory consolidation during sleep. Dreams, he explained, might be the hippocampus replaying emotionally significant recent memories at much faster rates, so that the rest of the brain could learn from experiences that had occurred only once in real life. It was a form of internal simulation—the brain training itself on synthetic data, running through scenarios while the body slept. The parallels to how AI systems learned were, for a neuroscientist turned AI researcher, almost unbearably resonant.

The question of what makes us unique—the question that had driven him since childhood—was not, for Hassabis, a sentimental one. It was a scientific question, and he believed it was answerable. Physics and neuroscience, he had long argued, were in some ways the most fundamental subjects: one was concerned with the external world out there, and the other with the internal world in our minds. Between them, they covered everything. And AI had the potential to help us understand both.

• • •

When asked what he would do after AGI—after the mission was complete, after the meta-solution had been built and deployed—Hassabis gave two answers, and both were revealing. The first was that he wanted to use AGI itself to help answer the deepest questions in physics: the nature of time, the origin of the universe, a fundamental theory that might unify quantum mechanics and gravity. This was the scientific dream—using the most powerful tool ever created to push the boundaries of human knowledge into domains that had resisted every previous approach.

The second answer was that he might go back to making games. He said it with a smile, but he was not joking. Games had been his first love. They had been the medium through which he had first encountered artificial intelligence, the domain in which he had built his earliest systems, the proving ground for the ideas that had led to AlphaGo and ultimately to the Nobel Prize. He dreamed about what he would have built in the nineties if he had access to the AI systems of today—open-world games where the narrative adapted dynamically, where the simulation was so rich that every playthrough was genuinely new. Perhaps, he admitted, the whole arc of his career—from Theme Park to AlphaGo to AlphaFold to Gemini—had been, subconsciously, a plan to build the tools that would one day let him make the ultimate game.

• • •

There is a through-line in the life of Demis Hassabis that is almost too neat to be true, and yet the evidence for it is overwhelming. A boy in Finchley buys a computer with his chess winnings and teaches himself to program. He designs games, programs AI, studies the brain, builds a company, teaches a machine to play Go, predicts the shape of every protein in the human body, wins the Nobel Prize, and then—when asked what he will do when all of it is done—says he might go back to making games. The circle closes. The infinite game continues.

At a chess tournament when he was eleven, watching the world's strongest players devote their extraordinary minds to moving wooden pieces across a board, Hassabis had felt something that would shape the rest of his life. It was not dissatisfaction with chess—he loved the game and would always love it. It was the sense that there was a higher use for all that brainpower. What if, instead of moving pieces, those minds were curing cancer? He stepped away from competitive chess. But he never stopped playing.

He had spent the next three decades building a machine that could think, and then pointing that machine at the problems that mattered most. Protein structures. Drug discovery. The physics of the world. And now, at the frontier, he was confronting the biggest problem of all: what it meant to be intelligent, what it meant to be conscious, what it meant to be human in a universe that was, he believed, fundamentally an informational system waiting to be understood.

The FT essay he had written in 2017—the essay that had given this book its title—ended with a sentence that served as both a prediction and a prayer. AI, he wrote, might one day help us attain a better understanding of what makes us unique, including shedding light on such enduring mysteries of the mind as dreaming, creativity, and perhaps one day even consciousness. If that happened, it might prove one of the greatest discoveries of them all.

He was forty-nine years old. The work was not done. It might never be done, because the game he was playing had no endpoint—only deeper levels, harder puzzles, more astonishing landscapes to explore. It was the game he had been playing since he was four years old, watching his father play his uncle and realizing, within two weeks, that he could beat the adults around him. The meta-solution was not a machine. It was a way of thinking about the world: that the universe was structured, that its patterns were discoverable, that intelligence was the key to everything else. The boy from Finchley had bet his life on that idea, and the universe, so far, was proving him right.

A Note on How This Book Was Written

No human wrote a single word of this manuscript.

Every sentence, every paragraph, every chapter of this book was generated by artificial intelligence. The primary author was Claude, made by Anthropic. The cross-reviewers were ChatGPT, made by OpenAI, and Gemini, made by Google DeepMind—the very company this book is about.

My role was that of an editor, a director, and occasionally a fact-checker of the fact-checkers. I provided the source material: interviews, podcasts, documentaries, lectures, and articles that I had spent months collecting. I shaped the structure, chose what to include, decided the tone, and pushed back when something did not feel right. But I did not write the words. The AI did.

The process was iterative and adversarial. Claude wrote each chapter, then conducted its own fact-check, verifying every claim against primary sources. Over five hundred individual claims were checked across the seventeen chapters. Errors were found and corrected—thirty-one in total, ranging from a misidentified Cambridge college to a conflated project name to an inexact rendering of a Nobel lecture. ChatGPT and Gemini then independently reviewed the full manuscript, each flagging issues the others had missed. Three competing AI systems, built by three competing companies, checking each other's work.

The result was a manuscript that is, I believe, more rigorously fact-checked than most traditionally authored biographies. Not because AI is infallible—it is not, as the thirty-one corrections attest—but because the process of using multiple models as adversarial reviewers catches errors that a single human author, working alone, almost certainly would not.

There is an irony here that I want to name directly. This is a book about a man who believes that artificial intelligence will become the meta-solution—the tool that helps us solve everything else. And the book itself was written by that tool. It is, in a small way, evidence for the thesis it describes.

I do not claim this makes the book better than one a skilled human biographer would have written. A human writer would have brought intuition, voice, and a lifetime of literary sensibility that no model yet possesses. What I do claim is that it makes this book possible in a way it would not have been five years ago, and that the quality of what AI can produce—when guided by a human who cares about getting it right—is now remarkable.

The future of writing is not human or machine. It is human and machine. This book is one of the earliest examples of what that collaboration looks like.

A note on language. This book is written in British English. Demis Hassabis grew up in North London. He went to Cambridge. He built DeepMind in King's Cross. The story is set, for most of its length, in England. I am British myself, and although I now live in California, it felt wrong to strip the text of the spellings and conventions that belong to the world it describes. So you will find "organised" rather than "organized," "behaviour" rather than "behavior," and "maths" rather than "math." American readers will have no trouble with any of it, and I hope the consistency lends the book a voice that suits its subject.

— *Paul Johnson, California, 2026*

About the Author

I first encountered Demis Hassabis the way millions of people did: through a video game. I was a kid in the English countryside, glued to a chunky PC, building roller coasters and burger stalls in Theme Park. I had no idea that the teenager who had helped design it was already thinking about artificial intelligence, or that his career would trace an arc from that game to the Nobel Prize. I just knew the game was brilliant.

Decades later, living in San Francisco, I found myself returning to the story. Not because of nostalgia, but because of recognition. I grew up in a small village in the UK with a dream of making it to Silicon Valley. In 2013, with no connections and no safety net, I moved to San Francisco to co-found Lemonaid Health, a telehealth company built on the belief that technology could make healthcare more accessible. Over eight years my team and I lived the roller coaster ride of running a startup (no longer in a video game). In 2021 I became a venture capitalist investing in AI startups.

The entrepreneurial journey is, at its core, a story about conviction: about believing something is possible before you have any evidence, about persuading other people to believe it too, and about enduring the years when it looks like it might not work. Hassabis had all of that, but at a scale and with stakes that dwarfed anything I had experienced. He was not trying to build a company. He was trying to build a mind.

What fascinated me most was the gap between how the world saw DeepMind—as a Google subsidiary, a research lab, a maker of game-playing programs—and what Hassabis was actually trying to do. The ambition was so large that most people simply could not see it. I wanted to write the book that made it visible: the human story behind the most consequential scientific project of our time.

I'm not a natural writer. In fact English was one of my weakest subjects at school. So this book was written by AI and I served as the director and editor.

— Paul Johnson, California, 2026

...

Paul Johnson is a British entrepreneur and venture capitalist based in San Francisco, California. He co-founded Lemonaid Health, which pioneered the consumerisation of telehealth in the United States and was acquired by 23andMe in 2021 for $400M. He invests in technology startups. He played Theme Park when he was nine and has never quite got over it.

Bibliography

This biography draws on fifty-two primary sources spanning 2010 to 2026, including long-form interviews, podcasts, documentaries, conference talks, academic lectures, and published profiles. The principal sources were the two Lex Fridman interviews (2021, 2025), Desert Island Discs (2017), the AlphaGo and Thinking Game documentaries, the Royal Society Mullard Award Lecture, the Nobel Prize phone call and ceremony, and joint sessions with Dario Amodei at the World Economic Forum and The Economist. Additional context was drawn from the Financial Times, Wired, Fortune, the Guardian, and Business Insider, as well as the relevant academic literature in Nature, Science, and the Proceedings of the National Academy of Sciences. Where dialogue or internal thoughts are attributed, they are drawn from the subject's own words in these recorded sources. No interviews were conducted by the author.

AlphaGo (2017). Documentary film directed by Greg Kohs. Moxie Pictures / Reel As Dirt.

The Thinking Game (2024). Documentary. Google DeepMind.

Hassabis, Demis. Nobel Prize Lecture: "Protein Structure Prediction with AlphaFold." Nobel Prize in Chemistry, Stockholm, December 2024.

Hassabis, Demis. Nobel Prize Phone Call Interview. Royal Swedish Academy of Sciences, October 2024.

Hassabis, Demis. Royal Society Mullard Award Lecture. The Royal Society, London, 2024.

Hassabis, Demis. Singularity Summit Talk. San Francisco, 2010.

Hassabis, Demis. TED Talk. Vancouver, 2024.

Hassabis, Demis. Interview by Alex Kantrowitz. Big Technology Podcast. May 2025.

Hassabis, Demis. Interview by Alex Kantrowitz. Big Technology Podcast. January 2026.

Hassabis, Demis. Interview by Hannah Fry. DeepMind: The Podcast, Episode 8. 2020.

Hassabis, Demis. Interview by Kirsty Young. Desert Island Discs. BBC Radio 4, 2017.

Hassabis, Demis. Interview by Lex Fridman. Lex Fridman Podcast, Episode 299. 2021.

Hassabis, Demis. Interview by Lex Fridman. Lex Fridman Podcast, Episode 475. July 2025.

Hassabis, Demis. Interview by Reid Hoffman. Possible Podcast: "AI, Game Theory, Multimodality, and the Nature of Creativity."

Hassabis, Demis. Interview with Chris Anderson. TED Interview Podcast. 2023.

Hassabis, Demis. Google DeepMind Podcast Season Finale: "The Future of Intelligence." December 2025.

Hassabis, Demis. Oreate AI Exclusive Interview. February 2026.

Hassabis, Demis, and Dario Amodei. Radio Davos: "The Day After AGI." World Economic Forum, January 2026.

Hassabis, Demis, and Dario Amodei. Joint interviews. The Economist. 2025–2026.

Hassabis, Demis, and Sergey Brin. Big Technology Podcast: "AI Scaling, AGI Timeline, Robotics, Simulation Theory." May 2025.

AlphaGo press conferences. Seoul, South Korea. March 2016.

Hassabis, Demis. Fortune Titans & Disruptors. World Economic Forum, Davos, January 2025.

Hassabis, Demis. Sources Live (Alex Kantrowitz). World Economic Forum, Davos, January 2025.

World Economic Forum Davos sessions featuring Hassabis. 2025–2026.

Gibbs, Samuel. "Demis Hassabis: 15 Facts About the DeepMind Technologies Founder." The Guardian, 28 January 2014.

Hassabis, Demis. "The Mind in the Machine: Demis Hassabis on Artificial Intelligence." Financial Times, 20 April 2017.

Shead, Sam. "The Incredible Life of DeepMind Founder Demis Hassabis." Business Insider.

Wired staff. "Inside DeepMind's Epic Mission to Solve Science's Trickiest Problem." Wired, 2017.

Mnih, Volodymyr, et al. "Human-Level Control Through Deep Reinforcement Learning." Nature 518 (2015): 529–533.

Silver, David, et al. "Mastering the Game of Go with Deep Neural Networks and Tree Search." Nature 529 (2016): 484–489.

Jumper, John, et al. "Highly Accurate Protein Structure Prediction with AlphaFold." Nature 596 (2021): 583–589.

Hassabis, Demis, et al. "Patients with Hippocampal Amnesia Cannot Imagine New Experiences." Proceedings of the National Academy of Sciences 104, no. 5 (2007): 1726–1731.

Isomorphic Labs. "Isomorphic Labs Announces $600 Million Funding." Press release, 31 March 2025.

Queen Elizabeth's School, Barnet. "Academic, Innovator & Entrepreneur: Demis Hassabis." School website.

Association for Computing Machinery. "David Silver to Receive 2019 ACM Prize in Computing." ACM Awards, 2020.

www.ingramcontent.com/pod-product-compliance
Lightning Source LLC
Chambersburg PA
CBHW020457160726
47991CB00007B/2690